MILITARY HISTORY
FROM PRIMARY SOURCES

THE
CRIMEAN
WAR

JAMES GRANT

EDITED AND INTRODUCED
BY BOB CARRUTHERS

Pen & Sword
MILITARY

This edition published in 2013 by
Pen & Sword Military
An imprint of
Pen & Sword Books Ltd
47 Church Street
Barnsley
South Yorkshire
S70 2AS

First published in Great Britain in 2012 in digital format by
Coda Books Ltd.

Copyright © Coda Books Ltd, 2012
Published under licence by Pen & Sword Books Ltd.

ISBN 978 1 78159 235 9

This book contains an extract from 'British Battles on Land and Sea' by James
Grant. Published by Cassell and Company Limited, 1894.

A CIP catalogue record for this book is
available from the British Library

Printed and bound by CPI Group (UK) Ltd, Croydon, CR0 4YY

Pen & Sword Books Ltd incorporates the Imprints of Pen & Sword Aviation, Pen
& Sword Family History, Pen & Sword Maritime, Pen & Sword Military, Pen
& Sword Discovery, Pen & Sword Politics, Pen & Sword Atlas, Pen & Sword
Archaeology, Wharncliffe Local History, Wharncliffe True Crime, Wharncliffe
Transport, Pen & Sword Select, Pen & Sword Military Classics, Leo Cooper, The
Praetorian Press, Claymore Press, Remember When, Seaforth Publishing and
Frontline Publishing

For a complete list of Pen & Sword titles please contact
PEN & SWORD BOOKS LIMITED
47 Church Street, Barnsley, South Yorkshire, S70 2AS, England
E-mail: enquiries@pen-and-sword.co.uk
Website: www.pen-and-sword.co.uk

CONTENTS

INTRODUCTION

James Grant was a prolific author who produced a huge volume of books on military and historical subjects in the latter half of the nineteenth century. The material here was first published in 1894, only 40 years after the end of the Crimean War, at a time when many of the participants were still in their sixties. Grant therefore had access to the primary source interviews which are now lost forever.

Originally published as part of the Cassell's series "*British Battles on Land and Sea*", it presents the reader with an intriguing insight into how contemporary writers addressed their subject. They say the past is another country and that is certainly true in this instance. Mr. Grant's work is clearly 'of its time' and reflects the attitudes of the day which were unashamedly xenophobic, jingoistic and militaristic. It nonetheless repays the reader with a unique window on the past, bringing the long lost world of Victorian Imperialism into focus.

The engravings and illustrations are late nineteenth century and are reproduced as close as possible to how they originally appeared. Not all the engravings were produced by eye witnesses, but they certainly were scrutinised by survivors of the campaign. The works of imagination depicting the brave Red Coats in the thick of the action are fairly obviously embroidered and romanticised, but the portraits, landscapes and depictions of everyday soldiering all have a period flavour which reflects that the events were still within living memory. These wonderful engravings provide a direct link with the past and together with Mr. Grant's period text produce an absorbing account of the Crimean War through Victorian eyes.

Bob Carruthers

BOARDMENT OF ODESSA, 1854

Since the battle of Waterloo, peace had reigned in Europe; but the 28th of March, 1854, saw Britain once more at war. The battles in Cabul and Central India were too remote in their influences and scene operation to kindle great national enthusiasm, and since the day of carnage around Mont St. Jean, ours had been a land of peace; but at the very time when Wellington, the hero of so many past glories, was being borne to his last home, by the side of Nelson, the nation could little foresee that the seeds of another conflict were germinating, and on Russian soil.

A petty dispute about what was called the custody of the Holy Places: the guardianship of the various churches and shrines in Jerusalem and Bethlehem, of which France became protector by a treaty in 1740, swelled by the degrees into a great aggression on the part of Russia, when, on the 5th of May, 1853, Prince Menschikoff presented an ultimatum, demanding the acknowledgement of a Russian protectorate over all Greek subjects of the Turkish Empire; an assertion of sovereignty over nearly four-fifths of its people. The obscure squabble between the priests of the rival churches in the Holy City thus suddenly became a vast European difficulty. Britain, Austria, France and Prussia, felt themselves bound to interference of the balance of power.

On the 26th June, the Emperor Nicholas announced his intention of occupying the Danubian principalities of Wallachia and Moldavia, as "material guarantees," and an army corps, under general Dannenberg, entered the latter state. Several attempts were made by the Western powers to arrange the growing quarrel; but the Sultan remained firm, after giving the Russian invaders fifteen days to evacuate the Principalities, Omar Pasha, a Croatian peasant, who had risen to be generalissimo of the Ottoman army, with a force of 120,00 strong, established his head-quarters at Shumla, awaiting the expiration of the guaranteed time, to oppose the large army that now occupied the two principalities.

On the 27th of March 1854. Queen Victoria, in a message to both Houses of parliament, stated that she "felt bound to afford active assistance to her ally, the Sultan, against unprovoked aggression;" and on the following day war was declared in the usual form, by the heralds of London and at Edinburgh. The Emperor napoleon also declared war. In anticipation of these declarations, which had long been deemed inevitable, our Mediterranean fleet had anchored outside the entrance of the Dardanelles, where it was soon joined by the French; and one of the most powerful squadrons that had ever left the British isles, led by old Sir Charles Napier, passed into the Baltic, there to threaten the great fortress of Russia, and await the tide of events.

Meanwhile, each country prepared an expeditionary army for the Eats, and the British contingent, physically and morally one of the most splendid armies that ever marched under the British colours, departed, under the command of Lord Raglan, for the seat of war. He was accompanied, as generals of division, by men whose names stood high in our military annals, and by brigadiers who were second to none in skill and bravery. In Britain, public feeling was greatly heightened by the production of the famous "Secret Correspondence," in which the ambitious Nicholas coolly proposed to us the partition of Turkey, and the division of that empire between himself and the Queen; and this honest indignation was in no way diminished, when it was discovered that exactly similar overtures had been made to France, and that in these Britain had been carefully kept out of the bargain. The entire mass of our people became unanimous for war; and for the first time since the Crusades, Britons and Frenchmen stood side by side as allies. Marshal St. Arnaud, resigning his post as Minister of War, led the French army; his second in command being General Canrobert, a native of Brittany, who had won the highest distinction during the wars in Algeria, at the head of the 3rd Light Infantry.

On the 3rd of January, 1854, the combined British and French fleet, under the command of Vice-Admiral Dundas, entered the Black Sea, and on the 22nd of April, there ensued the first great act in the terrible drama of the new war - the bombardment of Odessa, a city with fully a hundred thousand inhabitants, who are wont to boast of it as the "Russian Florence."

It lies on the western shore of a small bay of the Black Sea, between the mouths of the Dnieper and Dniester, and is entirely of modern erection. In the bay there is good holding-ground, and anchorage for the largest vessels, close to the shore. The city presents an imposing appearance when viewed from the seaward. The line of cliffs on, which the town stands, has a slight curve inwards, giving the bay a radius of three miles. These cliffs lace the north-east, and towards the north they sink into low sandy mounds and flat endless steppes. These cliffs are crowned by white buildings, many of which are classical in aspect, and rise over each other like the seats of an amphitheatre. Odessa is fortified in the most modern style, and has on its eastern side a citadel that commands the port.

A gigantic staircase, consisting of 200 steps, conducts from the very centre of the town downward to the beach. The aspect of its broad streets is white and glaring; clouds of dust are always whirling there, powdering alike the passengers and the rows of stumpy trees, till all are reduced to nearly the same colour as the houses; and off this place the combined fleet came to anchor, to resent an outrage.

The British official declaration of war had reached Admiral Dundas on the 9th of April, when at anchor in Baltschik Bay, near Varna. Upon this, H.M. steamer Furious was sent to Odessa to bring away our consul. She hove to with a flag of truce flying at her mast-head, and sent in a boat also displaying a flag of truce, to demand that official as a British subject. There was some delay in returning an answer, and the lieutenant in command of the boat deemed it right to return to the ship; upon which, the Russians, with the same treacherous spirit manifested by them at Hango, opened fire upon the boat, and in the direction of the steamer. Seven cannon-shot were discharged, but without effect.

On the 17th (the French official declaration of war, without which Admiral Hamelin was unwilling to act) both fleets sailed for Odessa, before which they came to anchor on the afternoon of the 20th.

Of General Osten-Sacken, the military governor, an explanation was demanded of his reason for outraging a flag of truce, an object held sacred by all civilised nations. The answer he sent was unsatisfactory, and what was worse still, untrue. He declared that his guns did not fire upon the boat, but upon the Furious, which he alleged "was steaming up the bay, heedless of customary signals, for the sole purpose of examining it;" whereas, the fact was, that she had remained hove to and motionless.

Upon this, they sent in a demand for the instant delivery of all the shipping in the port, adding that in the event of no answer arriving by sunset on the following day, they would terribly punish this outrage on the law of nations; and accordingly, on the morning of the 22nd, they commenced an attack -upon the Imperial Mole, which ended in its destruction, and that of most of the Russian ships within it.

Stretching out from below the cliffs we have described, at

the lower or southeast end of the town, runs a long fortified pier, at the end of which stood a lighthouse. This is called the Quarantine Mole, and it shelters a great fleet of ships belonging to all nations. Their crews are never permitted to enter Odessa, but are strictly confined within a walled enclosure, which is closely guarded. This place is at the foot of the cliffs, and there they are compelled to remain, even though their ships were six months in port. Under pretence of preserving Odessa from disease, the Russians have made this quarantine enclosure a source of hateful tyranny and most obnoxious to seamen.

At the time the combined fleets arrived, "this mercantile prison of all nations "was very full, and on the eventful morning of the 22nd of April every ship had her national colours at the main-mast head, as if appealing for succour, and protesting against cannon-balls, intended for the Russians, falling amongst them; there were the stars and stripes of America, the red and yellow colours of Spain, the crosses of Sweden and Norway, and so many more, that with such a Varied display of bunting streaming on the wind, the harbour of Odessa seemed as if decked for a festival rather than for a bombardment from the now enormous guns of modern war.

The attacking force had special orders to give this Mole as wide a berth as possible, so as to avoid any necessity for returning a fire in that quarter, and thus injuring the shipping of neutral powers within.

The following was the force detailed for the bombardment:

The British war-steamers Tiger (afterwards lost); Retribution, 28 guns; Sampson, 6; Terrible, 21; and Furious, 16; with the French steamers, Mogador, Vauban, Descartes, and Caton. There was a detachment of rocket-boats sent in advance, under Commodore Dixon; while our Sanspareil of 70 guns, and the Highflyer, 21 guns, acted as a reserve.

This force proceeded from the Quarantine Mole to another

9

Bombardment of Odessa

designated the Imperial Mole, which, at the northern extremity of the cliffs enclosed a wedged mass of Russian ships of every sort and size, and some large stores and barracks. Both of these moles displayed a most formidable array of embrasures for cannon, and there was a battery between them and the base of the cliffs; but all these seemed to be but indifferently armed.

The orders for the steamers were, "to go as far as possible in-shore, so as to rake and destroy the Imperial Mole; but to avoid firing upon any part of the town, or upon the shipping in the Quarantine Mole."

About twenty minutes to seven they began, the Sampson leading the way in gallant style. When within a proper distance from the shore, each war-steamer delivered the fire of her enormous guns, and then steered round in a circle of about half a mile in diameter; and thus they kept wheeling, as one who was present wrote, "like so many waltzers, without ever touching or getting into scrapes."

Steadily and rapidly did the great guns of the Mole answer; the cliffs that overhung the Bay of Odessa echoed their booming with a thousand reverberations; and, in the course of an hour, the French steamer Vauban came out towards the greater ships of both fleets, on fire from the effects of red-hot shot, and seriously riddled in several places. The flames were got under, and once more she steamed into her place in the fiery circle that poured death and destruction into Odessa. For a time the fire from the attacking squadron, which was terrific, failed to silence that from the seventy embrasures of the Mole; at length, the Russian cannonade became slow, though persistent

And regular, replying about once every two minutes, and towards two in the afternoon, a building of wood at the rear of the Tongue Battery caught fire and blew up.

The steamers continued to ply with shot and shell all the mass of shipping within the Mole, and these on every hand were sinking or sheeted with fire, when suddenly a new feature came in the bombardment. A battery of six-horse artillery guns came galloping down the beach, were unlimbered, wheeled round and opened a fire on the rocket-boats, which at that moment were within musket-shot of them.

Fortunately no one in Commodore Dixon's little division was struck, but a shower of balls fell amidst it, ploughing up the water in white spouts, and dashing the oars to pieces. On this, the rocket-boats and the steamers opened on the horse artillerymen, and soon sent them scampering with their guns, as fast as their horses could take them out of range, behind some houses, which, in a few minutes, the great rockets that went roaring from the boats sheeted with flames. Till five in the afternoon, the steamers kept up the bombardment.

In the early part of the day, while they were thus engaged, the British frigate Arethusa was ordered to attack the southern side of the Quarantine Mole, to divert the fire of its guns, which had proved very troublesome. This sailing frigate, one of the last of the true "wooden walls of old England," stood into the bay in beautiful style, cheered by the admiring seamen of the fleet as she did so. She delivered her fire, filled, tacked, and fired again, handled by her crew, as she would have been in the days of Nelson.

After a time, the breeze that had borne her in freshened; then, though under fire, the hands went aloft, and her topsails were reefed; but she was recalled by the admiral.

During the cannonading, several British merchantmen crept out of the Quarantine Mole, set their sails and escaped, their crews full of thankfulness to do so. The outrage on the flag of truce was severely punished, for a vast amount of Russian property, but chiefly that of the government, was destroyed. Though completely in our power, and at our mercy, the town and the neutral shipping were spared as much as possible.

Some of our steamers were injured by shot; but our loss was only one British seaman killed and eight or nine wounded - none of them severely. Another account says that the Terrible had two men killed and five wounded; the Retribution three, and the Sampson five.

The Terrible fired red-hot shot from her ten-inch guns, and it was through her cannonade that the shipping was set on fire and that the magazine was blown up. She was closer in shore than any of the other vessels. The burning of the shipping occupied forty-eight hours. A large Russian frigate that lay among them was blown up when the flames reached her powder-room.

At five, the admiral signalled the squadron to return to the anchorage from whence the crews of the line-of-battle ships had been eager spectators of this bombardment, the first that had taken place since Lord Exmouth's retributive visit to Algiers. The guns of the Arethusa destroyed a Russian barrack at a short distance from Odessa, on the sea-coast, and blew up its magazine. Each of the vessels which remained out of the action had sent a rocket-boat for firing twenty-four-pound rockets; and these dreadful missiles, as they rushed roaring through the air, caused terrible destruction where-ever they passed. The dockyard was the chief point to which they were launched. When the Imperial Mole was destroyed, and its magazine blown up, the fleet gave three cheers, the French commencing.

The Russian losses we never ascertained.

As the Terrible had distinguished herself most in this action, she was received with all honours as she passed through the fleet, and was loudly cheered as she steamed on her way to the Bosphorus. "She has suffered much in her personal appearance," says a print of the day; "her paddle-boxes are a good deal knocked about, and she has twelve shots in her hull. Captain McCleverty remained on a paddle-box all the time, and narrowly escaped a bullet."

It was the Empress Catherine II, who, after the Peace of Jassy and the cession of Bessarabia to ever-encroaching Russia, fixed upon this place - then called Khodjabey, and consisting of only a few houses - as a future sea emporium.

Many regiments were employed in the construction of those public works, which our guns destroyed.

The Emperor Alexander followed up the views of Catherine; and in 1804 an entrepot was established at Odessa, a name Italianised from Odessus, that first bestowed upon it by her.

After the bombardment of Odessa, the fleets left that part of the coast to cruise before Sebastopol.

CHAPTER II

BOMBARDMENT OF BOMARSUND, 1854

Though our army yet lay inactive in its camp at Varna, elsewhere the war was being waged with varying success. Our war steamer, the Tiger, ran ashore near Odessa, twenty days after the bombardment of that place, and was destroyed by the Russians, who took 200 of her crew prisoners. On the 17th of May, Silistria was besieged; but the Turks compelled the Russians to raise the blockade, and drove them across the Danube. Again they defeated the Russians at Giurgevo; but on the 30th of July they lost the battle of Bayazid in Armenia, and had 2,000 men slain. In the preceding month, H.M. steamers, the Firebrand and Fury, under Captain Parker, each carrying six heavy guns, utterly destroyed the Russian batteries at the Sulina mouth of the Danube, hear the Bessarabian village of the same name.

The Queen came to visit the fleet destined for the Baltic before its departure, and loud indeed were the cheers that greeted her; and equally loud and hearty were those that rang over the water, "when," to quote a spirited journalist, "Sir Charles Napier, 'Fighting Charlie,' came forward on the poop to bow his acknowledgments for the shouts of the thousands of spectators whose boats swarmed round the ship which bore the fortunes of Britain. In a fortnight, our admiral promised us that he would be in Cronstadt or in heaven; and we all cheered our hearts out in honour of the brave old sailor who was going forth conquering and to conquer, though the ships that sailed under Napier to the Baltic are now as much things of the past as if they had belonged to the days of triremes."

The first division of our Baltic fleet - a fleet such as even Nelson had never dreamed of - under Sir Charles Napier, sailed from Spithead on the nth of March. The second division followed on the 16th. In that month, the total strength of our naval force in the North Sea amounted to twelve line-of-battle ships, of which nine were screws and three sailing vessels; with sixteen frigates and corvettes, of which nine were screws and seven, paddle-wheeled steamers, making a total of twenty-eight ships, armed with 1,363 guns, their horsepower being 9,810, and their men 14,015 in number. On the 20th of April, the admiral, in the Valorous, was at Copenhagen; and we are told "the Danes were excessively pleased with him for taking off his hat on landing."

On the 28th, the Bulldog, a six-gun steamer, brought to him the important intelligence that war had been declared, and naturally the thoughts of all in the fleet were turned to the attack on Cronstadt; but during all his operations in the Baltic, the admiral was hampered and crippled by the timidity, or worse, of the ministry in London. He did not foresee that such would be the case, and on receiving the tidings brought by the Bulldog, he issued the following highly characteristic address by signal to his fleet: -

"Lads, war is declared! We are to meet a bold and numerous enemy. Should they offer us battle; you know how to dispose of them. Should they remain in port, we must try to get at them. Success depends upon the quickness and precision of your fire. Lads, sharpen your cutlasses, and the day is your own!"

This address elicited reiterated cheers from the crew of the Duke of Wellington, 131 guns, which carried the flag of the admiral, or "Old Charley," as the sailors loved to call him.

Admiral Plumridge, however, had the honour of seizing the first prizes taken during the war. Five Russian vessels, with their cargoes, were taken by his squadron, and the total value of the prizes taken in the Baltic, by the 29th of April, amounted to

£80,000. By that time, Napier had sealed up all the ports there, as effectually as the winter ice had done. One squadron hovered in sight of Windau, Liebau, and Polangen, in the Gulf of Livonia; another was in the Gulf of Riga, effectually blockading that port; a third kept watch and ward at the mouth of the Gulf of Finland. Thus, it was impossible for any Russian ship to break the strict blockade established over all the native ports, without having to run the gauntlet through the whole British fleet, with the chance of being taken after all by that of France at the mouth of the Baltic.

The total strength of the Russian fleet in that sea was supposed to be at least thirty sail of the line; and to meet it, if it came forth to battle, Sir Charles Napier had, ere long, an equal number of 1 first-class war vessels, and twenty smaller, carrying 2,393 guns and 32,114 seamen and marines, perhaps the most powerful fleet ever assembled in one sea.

During the naval campaign in the Baltic, Admiral Plumridge destroyed the dockyards at Uleaborg and Brahestad, in the upper part of the Gulf of Finland, giving to the flames 28,000 barrels of tar, and taking several of the gun-boats, which had been built to oppose us.

When the French fleet, under Admiral Parseval Deschenes, came into the Baltic, the united armaments amounted to 54 sail, manned by 29,150 officers and men. An advance was then confidently expected on Cronstadt; but the evil influences at home proved too strong, and none was ever made, beyond the appearance of the fleets in line of battle before that place on the 29th of June.

In June, the Anglo-French forces appeared off the fortress of Bomarsund, in the isle of Aland, the chief of that singular group, which gives its name to the little archipelago, at the entrance of the Gulf of Bothnia, and which consists of sixty isles, inhabited by Swedes, and two hundred that are merely desert rocks.

Besides the great Russian fortress, which is in Sund parish, the only other remarkable place in Aland, is Castelholm, situated on an insular rock of red granite at the extremity of a tongue of land; the ruinous chateau in which Eric XIV, son of Gustavus Vasa, was imprisoned in 1634. Formerly the Aland Isles had kings of their own; but in 1809, they were all ceded to Russia, to the fleets of which their safe and commodious harbours afforded excellent anchorage and shelter, when watching the Lake of Malar and the Swedish coasting trade.

When the main body of the united fleet menaced Cronstadt, a squadron made its way through the narrow waters of the Aland Isles, and bombarded Bomarsund, which was rapidly advancing to a state of strength, that would have made it another Sebastopol in the Baltic Sea.

On the 21st of June it was assailed by the Heckla, Captain Hall; the Valorous, Buckle, and the Odin, Captain Scott, paddle steamers, which approached the place by the difficult southerly passage. At five p.m. the first-named vessel opened a cannonade, and the conflict soon became general. The ships moved in a circle, pitching in their shot of ninety-six pounds' weight, and one hundred pound shells, with congreve rockets, which set the barracks and other buildings in flames.

About six o'clock, a small battery placed on the skirt of a dark pine wood, mounting six horse-artillery guns, supported by a body of sharpshooters, opened a hot fire upon the steamers, the cannon of which responded with terrible effect. Several bombs fell close in front of this battery, which upon two occasions, was deserted by its gunners in consequence'; the explosion of the one hundred pound shells occasioned a dreadful crash; but fresh men always rushed to the guns with incredible ardour and resolution, while the riflemen maintained a constant, but very ineffective fire.

A bomb with a burning fuzee fell upon the deck of the

Heckla, but a young midshipman named Lucas, with the greatest coolness and courage, lifted it up and flung it overboard, and it sunk hissing into the sea. By seven o'clock, the battery was deserted. The forts continued to fire, but their shot fell short of the shipping.

By ten at night the principal fortress was on fire, and the event was hailed by three cheers from the squadron; at the same moment, a mighty bomb from the Valorous fell through its roof and exploded. On this, Captain Hall threw out the signal, "Well done, Valorous!"

At one in the morning of the 22nd, the British ceased firing, weighed anchor, and steamed slowly through the western Rinne on their return to join the admiral. One man on board the Heckla and two on board the Odin were wounded; but none were killed.

On the 26th and 27th the place was bombarded again, and the fortifications were half destroyed, many of the garrison were slain, while our loss was small.

Leaving Cronstadt, the fleet appeared before Bomarsund a third time, in August, when the great and final attack was made. The fortress still consisted of a main-work flanked by high round towers of massive red granite, built nine feet thick, the stones being beautifully cut. These towers, which occupied very lofty situations, were each sixty yards in diameter; each had twenty-four guns - 18, 24, and 32-pounders - and each was roofed with iron. A semicircular, or half-moon battery, the base of which was almost washed by the water, had ninety-two guns run through a double row of square portholes, and worked in casemates, capable of containing 3,000 men. The place had a complete garrison under General Bodisco; it mounted 180 pieces of cannon, and was stored with provisions for two years.

With the fleet were now a combined force of 11,000 French and 1,000 British troops, brought in ships from Calais. The latter were under the command of Colonel Jones, of the East India

Company's College at Chatham, a veteran of the expedition to Walcheren and of the Peninsular war. The former were commanded by General Louis Baraguay-d'Hilliers, Marshal of France, a survivor of the terrible battle of Borodino, and of the retreat from Russia.

When this third expedition visited Bomarsund, the Aland summer was at its height, and all on board the fleet were impressed by the beauty of the woods of beech and alder, hazel, silver birch, and dark pine, by the cosy farm-houses of the thrifty Swedes, the whirling windmills, and the purity of the deep-blue water that sparkled among the rocky isles.

The troops landed in two divisions on a misty morning on the north and south in Sund parish, and seized the most important points of communication, forming a complete line of investment, with their flanks resting on the sea. The French disembarked at Tranvick Bay, near the islet of Oon, four miles south of the harbour; and the British in a pretty cove near Hulta.

Incident in the attack on Bomarsund

After some preliminary skirmishing, by daybreak on the 13th of August, the former got their guns into position, and fired the first cannon-shot from the landward; but their metal being only sixteen-pounders, they failed to make any breach. They had four mortars only, but these damaged the roof of the principal fort, in front of which the French sailing line-of-battle ship of Admiral Parseval Deschenes, the Inflexible, of 90 guns, with four British vessels, the Edinburgh, carrying the flag of Admiral Chads; the Blenheim, the Hogue, and the Ajax, all of 60 guns and screw-propelling power, took up a position; while a flying squadron of steamers among the islets, made the investment as complete by sea as it was by land.

So heavy was the cannonade, that the officer commanding in Fort Tsu pulled down the Russian Cross and hoisted a white flag in its place. The terms of capitulation offered him were declined, so again the firing was resumed.

On the morning of the 14th, Lieutenants Gigot and Gibon, of the French line, at the head of a body of volunteers, stormed the tower. The commandant of it was bayoneted in the conflict; thirty-two of his men were taken prisoners, the rest escaped, and then the place was pillaged by the British.

Nearly the whole of the previous night the principal fort cannonaded a mud battery, armed with only a ten-inch mortar; and all the while, amid the roar of cannon from ships and shore, was heard the musketry fire of the French Chasseurs. On the afternoon of the 14th the enemy sprang a mine under the captured Fort Tsu, into which, since its capture, they had been firing from the main fortress; and by this unexpected explosion many French soldiers perished.

The same evening saw our breaching guns, consisting of three thirty-two-pounders and four howitzers, within 750 yards of the tower called the

Nortike; and by dawn their booming pealed over the sea

and the echoing isles, as shot after shot went crashing into the granite front of the great round tower, rending and tearing its solid masonry, and throwing showers of dangerous splinters in every direction. Every bullet told with terrible effect The Russians fired briskly in reply, and by one of their shots, Mr. Wrottesley, of the Royal Engineers, fell mortally wounded, and expired as he was being borne to the rear out of range.

A breach was soon made by the guns of Commodore Preedy, of the British navy, though his sailors by over-exertion became quite exhausted. Their places, however, were well supplied by the Royal Marine Artillery, and soon the breach was reported practicable; but ere an assaulting force could be detailed, the white flag was hoisted on the Nortike, in token of surrender, and 120 grey-coated Russian soldiers came forth, looking pale, famished, and crest-fallen.

Thus fell the towers which were the outworks of the main fortification, which the block-ships with their enormous guns pounded at leisure, at the distance of three thousand yards, throwing their shot within the long barrack which formed a portion of the place. So great was the roar of cannon now, that many of our officers and men were deaf for days after; but once more the white flag appeared, in token that the Governor of Aland, General Bodisco, was about to surrender in person.

"We anchored at half-past nine o'clock," wrote an officer of the steam-frigate Leopard, which carried the flag of Admiral Plumridge, "and beat to quarters at forty minutes past nine. The admiral now came down to the main-deck, and made a short speech to the men, who all fought in nothing but their trousers and a sleeveless flannel. Fire! and a broadside from the ship went slap into the devoted fort. A few trees intervened between us, so we could only see the roof."

The Leopard, he tells us, threw in a terrible fire of shells from her six main-deck guns, which were 32, 68, and 84-pounders.

She received twelve shots in return through her hull, and came out of the action with her main-top-mast shot away; she had two shot-holes in her funnel, through which the smoke was rolling half-way up.

Soon after the appearance of the white flag, which caused an immediate cessation of firing, General Baraguay d'Hilliers, a venerable-looking ' officer, with flowing, silvery hair, General Niel, and Brigadier Jones, with the admiral, repaired to the gate, and courteously received the Russian General Bodisco, who marched out at the head of 2,300 men, chiefly of the Finland Regiment, or 10th of the Imperial Line. Most of these men were native-born Finns; but among them were several convicts destined for Siberia, and these had to be separated from the rest.

Among the prisoners was a tall and stately-looking Pole, wearing a decoration, and who - as if disdaining the company amid which he found himself - marched alone to the beach; when, at five next morning, all that were taken were placed on board H.M.S. Hannibal, the officers requested and obtained permission to write farewell letters to their friends in Russia, as they had prospect of, perhaps, a long captivity before them.

They were also permitted to bring their wives and families with them. About fifteen thousand sterling, in silver roubles, was found in the military chest.

Thus fell these once formidable defences of the Aland Isles: the Boomar battered to pieces; the Nortike breached, and the Tsu Tower rent by the exploded mine. The former was undermined and destroyed on the 2nd of September. By six successive shocks, it was ultimately lifted up bodily, and thrown in ten thousand fragments over the isle. Prior to this, the place had been pillaged by the land and sea forces, and everything of value was carried away.

The Allied losses were only 53 killed and 86 wounded; but those of the Russians were estimated at 600 men killed alone.

ALMA, 1854

During the hot and breathless months of the Bulgarian summer, our splendid army lay inactive and literally rotting at Varna, as if only waiting for winter to commence the terrible game of war in hardy Russia, the land of ice and snow, and whose emperor boasted that her two greatest generals were January and February. Cholera decimated the army, and hundreds of brave fellows who had left the shores of Britain high in hope and the strength of manhood, found their graves in the beautiful valley of Aladyn, or on the hills that overlook the bleak and white-washed walls of Varna. The 7th, 23rd, and 88th Regiments, and all the infantry generally, suffered severely, except the Highland battalions, whose peculiar costume, by its warmth round the loins, is a species of safeguard against cholera.

The Inniskillings and 5th Dragoon Guards were reduced almost to skeletons, and few of our cavalry corps could muster more than 250 swords. Murmurs, not loud, but deep, were heard in the camp, where every heart burned to meet the enemy; and with joy the army quitted Varna and the Valley of the Plague on the 5th of September, and the 14th of the same month saw it landing in the Crimea, near the Lake of Kamishlu, some miles north of the Bulganak River, at a place where the beach was overhung by cliffs a hundred feet in height.

This great event took place on the anniversary of the death of the Duke of Wellington.

Save a boat-load of Zouaves being run down by a steam-transport, there was no accident. The morning was fine, and the surface of the Euxine was smooth as a mirror. The whole of the troops of the light division were first in the boats, in marching order, with sixty rounds per man; each sat with his musket between his knees, packed close; the seamen with their oars out in the rowlocks, all silent - all motionless and all awaiting the signal.

It was given, and a gleam seemed to pass over the burnished arms as the oars fell plashing into the water, and the whole line of boats, a mile in length, shot off from the fleet. At half-past eight, the first boat, which belonged to the Britannia, landed her detachment. Standing mid-leg in the water, the seamen assisted the troops in getting ashore, and rapidly Guardsmen and Linesmen, Fusiliers and Highlanders, Rifles, Lancers and Hussars, were seen forming by regiments on the beach.

Under Marshal St. Amaud and General Canrobert, the French were landing elsewhere, and ere long more than 60,000 men were under the colours, in Crim-Tartary - of old, the Isle of Kaffa. Our army was without baggage, and everything that might hinder an advance, thus it bivouacked on the bare ground, on the night of the 14th of September. The drenching rain came down in torrents, and the meagre uniforms, the blankets and greatcoats, speedily became soaked and sodden; but all ranks suffered alike, and the Duke of Cambridge strove to sleep amid his staff, with his head protected from the plashing wet by a little tilt-cart; but the effects of this endurance were speedily seen in the men of our young, and, as yet, untried army.

Some of our regiments took their ground on a hill, which rose near the landing-place, where they formed contiguous close columns of battalions, and these were still posted when the evening of the 14th closed. "But," says one who was present, "what were those long strings of soldiery now beginning to come down the hill-side and wind their way back to the beach? And what were those white burdens carried horizontally by the men? Already - already on this same day! Yes, sickness still clung to the army. Of those who only this morning ascended the hill with seeming alacrity, many now came down thus sadly borne by their comrades. They were carried on ambulance stretchers, and a blanket was over them. Those whose faces remained uncovered were still alive. Those whose faces had been covered by their blankets were dead. Near the foot of the hill the men began to dig graves."

And thus grimly was our war in the Crimea inaugurated by suffering and sudden death. The red-tapeism and ignorance of the authorities in London had much to do with all this; for we had learned nothing in the mode of conducting war since the days of Waterloo.

The British contingent, under Lord Raglan, consisted of 26,000 infantry and 1,000 cavalry with 60 pieces of cannon, divided into five divisions of foot and one of horse; the French mustered 30,000; and the Turks some 7,000 bayonets. The numbers as given by Dr. Russell, are 27,000 British, 23,000 French; and of the Russians, 33,000 or 34,000 in position at the Alma.

Varna

The Duke of Cambridge led the 1st division, which was composed of the Grenadier, Coldstream, and Scots Fusilier Guards, with Sir Colin Campbell's Highland brigade - the Black Watch, the Cameron and Sutherland Highlanders; hence it was deemed the *corps d'élite* of the army. The Earl of Lucan, who in his youth had served as a volunteer with the Russians, under Marshal Diebitch, in the campaigns against the Turks, led our slender division of cavalry - those splendid dragoons who were yet to be covered with glory by their charge through the Valley of Death.

The Quartermaster-General was Sir Richard Airey, K.C.B., and an officer who, from the first, had seen the necessity for procuring the means of transport, and whose aide-de-camp, when exploring, as the armies were advancing, was fortunate enough to come upon a Russian convoy, consisting of eighty wagons of flour, all of which he captured, and put their escort to rout.

It was on the morning of the 19th, that the march towards the enemy began, and our troops quitted ground that was perilous; for had the Russians come suddenly upon them, a battle must have beer* fought with our rear to the cliffs, where the Euxine rolled a hundred feet below, and where there could be no retreating; but as St Arnaud and his Frenchmen had assumed the honour of holding the right wing, they were permitted to keep it; the risk to them was thus greater, as in the advance the sea was always on their flank.

It was known that the enemy was somewhere in front, and every heart was full of expectation when the march began. The 11th Hussars and 14th Light Dragoons, under Lord Cardigan, formed the advanced guard. In their rear moved a body of the dark green Rifles in extended order.

After a two hours' halt, "we proceeded a distance of about ten miles further," says a surgeon of the Guards in his published diary; "rather a trying march for the men debilitated by the Bulgarian summer and by confinement on board ship. Towards the termination of our move to-day, therefore, they fell out, exhausted, in large numbers."

Yet in many corps the bands were playing, and the Highland war-pipes swelled upon the ear at times. The colours were all uncased and flying upon the light breeze that came from the blue Euxine, from whence, high into the cloudless sky, ascended the smoke of the steam-fleet, which came moving in unison with the army, far away on the right flank of the French.

But the music died away, and the spirit of the men seemed to sink as the hot and breathless day wore on. The Foot Guards seemed to suffer most from heat and thirst. Jackets were torn open; stocks and bearskins were cast aside. Many were seen by the wayside, speechless, choking, and writhing in agony. At last was reached the Bulganak River, where the troops were to bivouac for the night. The moment they came in sight of the

The Heights of Alma

cool stream that rippled between its green banks, and beautiful groves of olive and pomegranate trees, the troops burst from their ranks with shouts, and rushed forward to slake their burning and agonising thirst.

"In one brigade a stronger governance was maintained," says Kinglake in his "Invasion of the Crimea." "Sir Colin Campbell would not allow even the rage of thirst to loosen the high discipline of his splendid Highland regiments. He halted them a little before they reached the stream, and so ordered it, that by being saved from the confusion that would have been wrought by their own wild haste, they gained in comfort, and knew that they were the gainers. When men toil in organised masses, they owe what well-being they have to wise and firm commanders."

There, by the Bulganak, the troops bivouacked for the night.

On the eventful 20th, at four in the morning, while darkness reigned on land and sea, and the dew lay deep on everything, the troops got under arms, and after waiting till nine o'clock, to enable the generals to reconnoitre, the Allies were in full march once more, to force the Russians from their position on the heights of Alma.

The day proved bright and sunny, and a five miles' march brought the Allies in sight of the entrenched position of the enemy. High on the southern bank of the Alma, a river which rises on the western slope of the Chatyrdagh Mountain is a ridge of picturesque rocks, which terminate in a cliff that overhangs the Euxine. In the ravines of those rocks grew groves of turpentine and other trees, many of which had been felled to form abatis to encumber the advance of our troops. Along that ridge, two miles in length, were formed the lines of the Russians, and by the aid of field-glasses, their flat caps or spike-helmets, their grey-coated masses and glittering bayonets, could be discerned as the allied columns came on.

The cliff above the sea is lofty and precipitous; at its foot, sloping towards the river on one side, were extensive vineyards. About two miles from the mouth of the Alma was situated the Tartar village of Bourliouk, where a small bridge of wood crossed the stream. This village was set on fire by the Russians as we came on.

Their position was certainly one of vast strength. Deep trenches had been dug in the slope of the rocky ridge, and behind these were ranged their dense battalions of infantry. Redoubts and breastworks had been thrown up, and on the Kourgane Hill, 600 feet above the Alma, to protect his right; Menschikoff had constructed an enormous triangular battery, mounted with heavy cannon and twenty-four-pound howitzers.

The ascent to this battery was commanded by three others, mounting twenty-five guns. On the left of this position, crowning the high sea-cliff, a large redoubt had been commenced, but was unfinished on the day of the battle. The broken ground sloping towards the river was occupied by swarms of riflemen, who were ambushed among the green vineyards and thick leafy plantations in the deep ravines.

Thus situated, in one of the strongest natural positions ever occupied by an army, their left resting on a range of lofty cliffs scarcely accessible to the most active pedestrians, their line stretching across a range of hills strongly fortified, their right occupying, as we have said, a lofty eminence; the Russians confidently anticipated that the invaders, if not fully routed, would be completely checked until the arrival in the Crimea of more imperial troops; and, as a proof of this, in a letter to the emperor, a copy of which was found in his carriage after the battle, Prince Menschikoff expressed his assurance of being able to hold the heights of the Alma against all comers for at least three weeks.

In the heart of the great column of Kazan infantry on the

Kourgane Hill was borne the holy image of St. Sergius, to ensure victory, and in their rear were trains of carriages full of beautifully-dressed ladies from Sebastopol and Bagtche-Serai, "the Seraglio of Gardens," waiting, in a flutter of excitement, to see the defeat of "the island curs," as they termed the British, whom, curiously enough, they believed to be seamen dressed up in red coats, and incapable of withstanding the soldiery of "Holy Mother Russia."

A peculiar fragrance filled the morning air. It came from the leaves of a little aromatic herb (which there grows wild in vast quantities), when bruised by the feet of the marching columns, or the wheels of the field-artillery; and many places were covered by orange-coloured crocuses, growing thick as buttercups in the fields at home.

At last, the enemy was in front, and after forty years of peace, the great nations of Europe were once more meeting for battle!

It was during a pause before the engagement that, as Kinglake tells us, Sir Colin Campbell, in his grave, quiet way, said to one of his officers, "'This will be a good time for the men to get loose half their cartridges.' And when the command travelled along the ranks of the Highlanders it lit up the faces of the men, one after another, assuring them that now, at length, and after long expectance, they indeed would go into action. They began obeying the order, and with becoming joy, for they came of a warlike race; yet not without emotions of a grave kind, for they were young soldiers, and new to battle."

At half-past twelve the French steamers began to shell the heights from the seaward, and for about an hour and a half did much execution, while the Russians replied by a very inefficient fire. One shell fell neatly into an ambuscade which they had prepared for the advancing French, and when the smoke of its explosion cleared away, the prostrate forms of many mangled riflemen attested how severely it had done its work. At length

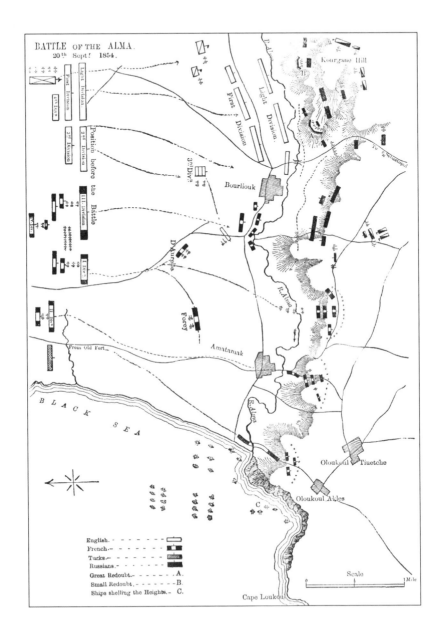

BATTLE OF THE ALMA.
20th Sept! 1854.

Light Division
First Division
4th Line
2nd Division

Position before the Battle
III. Division
1st Line
Line 2

II. Div"
From Old Fort

First Division
Light Division
3rd Div!
Bourliouk

D'Aurelle
R. Alma
To Sevastopol

Forey
Amatamak
R. Alma

Kourgane Hill

BLACK SEA

Oloukoul Tiuetche

Oloukoul Akles

C

English. — — — —
French. — — — —
Turks. — — — —
Russians. — — — —
Great Redoubt. — — — A.
Small Redoubt. — — — B.
Ships shelling the Heights. — C.

Scale
0   1 Mile

Cape Loukoul

32

the enemy fell back from the cliffs, and confined their efforts to the defence of the gullies beyond the fire of the steamers.

Meanwhile, the allied generals, one of whom - St. Arnaud - had taken the field in an almost dying condition, were steadily arranging their plan of attack. The extreme right of their line was composed entirely of the French troops - Zouaves, fresh from Algeria - and to them was assigned the task of scaling the cliffs and turning the enemy's left.

Sir De Lacy Evans, with the 2nd Division, formed of the 30th, 55th, 41st, 47th, and 49th Regiments, occupied the right of the British line, and joined the French left.

The left of our position was assigned to Sir George Brown's light division, composed of the 7th, 19th, 23rd, 33rd, 77th, and 88th Regiments, supported by that of the Duke of Cambridge, composed of the Guards and Highlanders.

The 3rd Division, under Sir Richard England, composed of the 38th, 50th, 1st Royal Scots, 4th, 44th, 28th, and 63rd, supported General Evans; while the 4th Division, consisting of the 20th, 21st, 63rd, 57th and the 1st battalion Rifle Brigade, with our small force of cavalry, formed a reserve to oppose a cloud of Cossacks who threatened our rear.

The French commenced the attack, and during their operations our infantry lay down - but in order of battle - under the enemy's fire. Through the Alma they dashed against the steep cliffs, under a terrific shower of round shot, grape, and musketry, which shrouded the whole face of the heights with clouds of white smoke, streaked with flashes of red fire, rousing the echoes in every hollow and ravine, and up they swarmed in yelling and impetuous masses.

The fierce little Zouaves, fresh from conquests in Africa - in their blue jackets, red breeches, and turbans - though hundreds fell on every hand, were seen to scale the heights at the point of the bayonet, and then, forming in two lines, to rush on the astonished Russians, whose general, being thus outflanked where he least expected, by having the cliffs carried, sought, but in vain, to change his front, and hurl back the French from the position they had won so speedily, so bravely, and with such awful loss.

The Russians in that quarter now fell back on the main army, but not without leaving hundreds of dead riflemen to attest the prowess of their antagonists.

The British infantry advanced into action at half-past one o'clock. The order flew along the line like lightning, for it was borne by the fiery and gallant Nolan. In the centre of our position was the still flaming village of Bourliouk, from the full stackyards of which smoke rose high into the air.

To the right of it two regiments of Adams's brigade, the 41st Welsh (so called since 1831) and the 49th, or Hertfordshire, crossed the Alma by a deep and perilous ford, under a galling fire from the Russian Minié Riflemen, who were ambushed among the vineyards on the opposite bank. The remainder, under Major-General Pennefather, crossed on the left of Bourliouk, and rapidly forming beyond it, the whole of Evans's division found itself engaged in a close and murderous strife.

"The first man killed," says Russell, "was a drummer, who was carrying a litter, and who was struck by a round shot, which bounded slowly along the road and hit him, with a peculiar squashing sound, on the hip. He fell, broken in two, and never moved again."

On the extreme left of the British advance the light division, under Sir George Brown, a Peninsular veteran, who had carried the colours of the 43rd at Copenhagen, and been wounded at Talavera, crossed the stream in their immediate front. Above them rose the rugged and precipitous banks, which were so steep in some places, that one of our officers, when in the act of climbing, had his spinal column traversed by a ball, fired downwards from the Russian ranks above. The thick vineyards, with their intertwisted branches and tendrils, and the abatis of felled trees, partially obstructed the advance of our splendid Light division; but nothing could surpass the coolness and resolution of the Royal and Welsh Fusiliers, of the 33rd, 19th, 77th, and Connaught Rangers, as they swept forward under the volleying fire, pausing only at times to snatch at bunches of the delicious Crimean grapes to quench their burning thirst.

Like hail the Minié balls were showered upon them. On every hand our men were falling fast; caps and epaulets, ears and fingers, were torn off; loud hurrahs mingled with the shrieks of the wounded; and cries of "Forward! on - on-forward!" and on their officers led them, waving their swords in front.

"Forward, the Welsh Fusiliers!" "On, Nineteenth!" "On, Seventy-seventh!" "Well done, Eighty-eighth!" Such were the shouts that rang on every side as the scarlet tide pressed upward, and too often with "the death-cry drowning in the battle's roar." The Light division swept on with such impetuosity, that it carried with it the whole 95th Regiment, which belonged to the second corps.

They formed line beyond the broken ground rapidly and magnificently, and threw their steady fire into the strong redoubts. Fast fell the dead, and faster still the wounded; and now commenced that most memorable up-hill charge by which we ultimately won the Alma.

Though half seen, half lost at times, old Sir George Brown was conspicuous on a grey horse at the head of his division. A sheet of lead tore through the Royal Fusiliers led by Lacy Yeo; they wavered for a moment - but a moment only - and, reforming, continued to advance. By the same fire were the Welsh Fusiliers decimated; and here we cannot do better than quote a well-written letter by one of the corporals named Harwood.

"The 23rd was in the Light division, covered by two

companies of the Rifle Brigade. We crossed a vineyard, and were led by Colonel Chester through the river, the opposite bank of which was very steep. The brave colonel went with us - we all shared alike; and as we clambered out, the enemy gave us a fierce fire, the cannon belching forth murderous volleys of grape and round shot, while musket-balls fell thick as hail. The men fell dead and wounded before me and at my side. They fell in every direction; yet, mechanically, I pressed onward, untouched. Up the hill we went with the Rifles, and half-way up the heights we reached the cannons' mouths, which were planted on the entrenchment. Our regiment was about to cross the stockade into the enemy's position, when the commands were given, 'Cease firing - retire!' because we were in danger of firing on the French. Our colonel rushed in front of us, shouting, ' No, no! - On, lads, on!' He fell with the word on his lips; and never spoke or raised his head again." "He lay dead," says Russell, "with a scornful frown, his sword clutched in the death-grasp." His horse was also killed.

Relief after relief was shot down under the colours of the 7th; one was lost for a time, but was found safe among the Royal Welsh. Under the colours of the latter, Lieutenant Anstruther (son of Sir R. Anstruther, of Balcaskie) fell dead; but it was snatched from his hand by a private named Lewis, who bore it waving towards the Great Redoubt.

Many of the wounded when limping or crawling to the rear, were again struck by Russian bullets, and sank to rise no more. On crossed muskets and dripping stretchers vast numbers of officers and men were borne, reeking in blood, to the river's edge for shelter. But still the human tide rolled up the hill, for nothing could withstand our glorious infantry. While in the act of crying, "Hurrah for the Royal Welsh! I shall remember you! "old Sir George Brown fell, amid a cloud of smoke and dust. He was supposed to be slain; an idea which for an instant paralysed the advance; but, springing to his feet, he once more led the charge, and, dashing onward, entered the Great Redoubt at the head of a mingled tide composed of the men of several regiments, reckless of the fire that tore through them from grey-coated masses in front.

A rifleman called Hugh Hannan assisted the general to remount, and under the murderous fire that was breaking the regiment to fragments, coolly saluted him, and said, "Are your stirrups the right length, sir?"

The flashing bayonets were lowered - man seemed to seek man, and the dead and dying were heaped over each other, trampled on, and smothered in blood.

The melee in the Great Redoubt was a most dreadful one; goo of our men and officers had now fallen in it and all up the rocky slope that led thereto. The colours of the Royal Welsh were flying above it, yet the victory was not won.

The British officers were evidently picked out by the Russians, their dress being easily remarked; while on the other hand, the uniform of the Russian officers so closely resembled that of the men, as to be almost indistinguishable, some small stars on the coat being the only distinction between them. Descending from the higher hills, a mighty column of Russian infantry, bearing with it the image of St. Sergius, a solemn trust, given by the Bishop of Moscow, and which had been borne in the wars of Alexis, of Peter the Great, and Alexander I., came rushing on now, with the miraculous assurance of victory.

They followed up a withering volley with a powerful bayonet charge. Then our troops at the redoubt, exhausted by their toilsome up-hill charge, began to waver and fall back before the yelling Russian hordes, who had a perfect belief in their own invincibility, and who barbarously bayoneted all our wounded as they came on, after deploying into line.

This temporary repulse proved terribly fatal to the Welsh

Fusiliers, who lost nine of their officers, and to the 33rd, among whom no less than nineteen sergeants fell, chiefly in defence of the colours and fourteen bullet-holes in one standard, and eleven in the other, attested the fury of the conflict. "The vindictive spirit of the enemy was, I think, as great as unexpected," says Dr. Robinson, of the Scots Fusilier Guards, in his Diary. "Many of our officers and privates met with their death-wounds whilst lying on the ground only slightly injured, the Russians, even though maimed themselves, firing deliberately on our disabled men. To this brutal disregard of the usages of civilised warfare, poor Lord Chewton of my regiment owed his death, and Colonel Haygarth the imminent danger of his life, whilst disabled, an attempt was made deliberately to shoot him through the head, by placing the muzzle of a firelock close to his face. His hand, instinctively raised, partly turned the course of the ball, and caused an extensive laceration of the scalp, in place of immediate death."

Death of Ensign Anstruther

In many instances, the Russians hewed off the fingers of those they murdered, in their haste and eagerness to possess the rings they wore.

Throwing open his ranks to allow the disordered regiments to re-form and recover breath, the Duke of Cambridge now brought up his division; but "once, when the sheets of fire from the redoubt seemed to threaten to sweep the battalions from the field, he gave the word to pause and re-form the line. Sir Colin Campbell, the gallant chief of the Highland Brigade, interposed, and the duke immediately recalled the order."

According to Kinglake, there was a momentary fear of the success of the duke's division, for an officer high in rank exclaimed, "The brigade of Guards will be destroyed! Ought it not to fall back?"

"Better that every man of Her Majesty's Guards should lie dead upon the field than turn their backs upon the enemy!" was the stern remark of the grand old veteran, Colin Campbell, as he galloped off to put himself at the head of his Highlanders, whom he was bringing on in echelon of regiments. They had reserved their fire, and were advancing in solemn silence.

When the Guards advanced into action, the fight for the standards of the Scots Fusiliers was a memorable struggle. Lieutenants Thistlethwayte and Lindsay, who bore them, literally hewed their way through the enemy; and though the staff of one was broken, and sixteen bullet-holes attested the fury of the conflict, and the colour-sergeants had fallen, pierced with balls, these officers bore their colours in triumph to the top of the hill.

The Duke of Cambridge had his horse shot under him.

Lieutenant Thistlethwayte afterwards died in what was not inaptly named by our men the "Bloody Hospital of Scutari."

Our fine brigade of Guards was severely cut up when the Highlanders drew near, and then, as Kinglake tells us, a man

Advance of the Highlanders at the Alma

in one of the regiments reforming on the slope cried in the deep and honest bitterness of his heart, "Let the Scotsmen go on: they'll do the work!" and with his three kilted battalions, Sir Colin, whose horse was shot under him, advanced to meet twelve of the enemy.

"Now, men," said he, "you are going into action; and remember this, that whoever is wounded - I don't care what his rank is - must lie where he falls. No soldier must carry off wounded men. If any man does such a thing, his name shall be stuck up in his parish kirk. Be steady - keep silence - fire low! Now men, the army is watching us I make me proud of my Highland Brigade!"

So beautifully does the author of "Eothen" - an eyewitness of this part of the battle - describe their movements, that we cannot resist quoting him again.

"The ground they had to ascend was a good deal more steep and broken than the slope close beneath the redoubt. In the land where those Scots were bred there are shadows of sailing clouds skimming up the mountain-side, and their paths are rugged and steep; yet their course is smooth, easy, and swift. Smoothly, easily, and swiftly the Black Watch seemed to glide up the hill. A few instants before, and their tartans ranged dark in the valley; now their plumes were on the crest."

Another line came on in echelon, and another still - the Cameron and the Sutherland Highlanders. And now, to the eyes of the superstitious Russians, the strange uniforms of those bare-kneed troops seemed novel, and even terrible; their white, waving sporrans were taken for the heads of low horses; and they cried to each other that the angel of light had departed, and that the demon of death had come.

A close and deadly fire was now poured into these "grey blocks," as Russell calls the Russian squares. No particular sound followed, save the yells of the wounded, while the

Highlanders "cast about" to reload; but after their next volley a strange rattling noise was heard, as the bullets fell like rain among the tin canteens and kettles which the enemy carried outside their knapsacks, for they were all right-about-face now.

A wail of despair floated over those grey-coated masses of Muscovite infantry as they broke and fled, throwing away muskets, knapsacks, and everything that might encumber their flight; and now for the first time rose the Highland cheer.

"Then," says the brilliant historian of the war, "along the Kourgane slopes and thence west almost home to the causeway, the hill-sides were made to resound with that joyous and assuring cry which is the natural utterance of a northern people so long as it is warlike and free."

The heights of the Alma were won, but 3,300 of the Allies lay killed and wounded on their green slopes, which were dotted for miles by spots in scarlet, blue, or grey, each spot a human corpse, or a man in mortal agony. Three Russian generals, 700 prisoners, and 750 of their wounded remained in our hands, according to Kinglake, though some authorities make them many more.

The moment the Russians gave way, our small force of cavalry, who had been most impatient onlookers of the fight, dashed through the river, without Lord Raglan's authority; and though the overturning of a field-gun, and the treacherous nature of the ford, caused some delay, they reached the Kourgane Hill soon after the Highlanders had swept it of the foe. They had six guns with them, and the fire of these told with fearful effect upon the retreating columns of the Russians. The battery was divided, one half of our cavalry, led by Lord Cardigan, escorting three guns on the right, while Lord Lucan, with the rest, escorted three on the left, and gleaned up many prisoners, who, as they were brought to the rear, were reviled and execrated by our wounded; for on all hands were now heard stories of Russian treachery and barbarity; and amid these, the fate of the Eddingtons was the most prominent.

"You have heard of the melancholy deaths of poor Captain and Lieutenant Eddington, of the 95th," says a medical officer, in his letter from the field. "They were brothers, and so attached to each other that the whole regiment respected them - I might rather say, loved them. Lieutenant Eddington exchanged into the 95th a few months ago, that he might share danger and risk death by his brother's side. Captain Eddington fell first, with a ball in his chest, and was left for a few moments on the hill-side while the regiment, which had been thrown into disorder, fell back to reform; and the whole troops witnessed his brutal murder. A Russian rifleman knelt down beside him, and while pretending to raise his canteen to the wounded man's lips, deliberately blew his brains out! A shout of rage and hatred burst from the whole regiment, and at the same moment they again charged up the hill, Lieutenant Eddington many yards in advance, crying for the men to follow him, and apparently mad with grief and excitement. He fell beneath a perfect storm of grape-shot and rifle-balls. His breast was absolutely riddled. The same grave holds them both; and their spirits, let us hope, have entered upon an eternal peace in the presence of God."

The French losses are estimated at 1,343 of all ranks; and their brave commander, Marshal St. Arnaud, who literally, as has been said, took the field in a dying state, after being twelve hours in his saddle, six days subsequent to the victory resigned the command to General Canrobert; and three days after that, he died on board the Berthollet, in which he had embarked for France.

Had our cavalry force been stronger, the losses of the enemy must have been greater. Worn out with the contest, our infantry were unable to pursue the retreating Russians, who fled in the direction of Bagtche-serai, where Prince Menschikoff hoped to recover from the shock of his defeat. Thus, after a fiery conflict of three hours, was the field of Alma won. That night the victorious armies bivouacked on the field.

Men who had been wounded in the fight crawled out of it to the surgeons, and, after having their wounds dressed, crawled back again to view the struggle in which they could no longer share. An officer who had a foot amputated was heard calling for his horse, that he might ride into the fray once more; so true it was that forty years of European peace had not weakened the old British spirit which won us the battles and the glories of the days of other years.

Our surgeons were wholly inadequate in number for the discharge of their duties; and so base was the parsimony of the British government, that, as one of them states in a published letter, on board the Kangaroo hospital ship "there were not necessaries for five out of fifty sufferers."

For two nights and days, without sleep or rest, did these devoted men labour to assuage the agonies of the wounded, some of whom were carried to the hospital by their comrades, while others, unaided, dragged their shattered limbs from the field of battle. Our men moved about, from their own scanty supply quenching the thirst of those who were past even speech. No dying enemy besought a draught in vain. Some, to quote "Voices from the Ranks," to their lasting shame be it said, drained the proffered flask, and then, summoning a last energy, discharged their muskets at their benefactors. Maddened by such foul ingratitude, our soldiers dashed out their brains by their clubbed muskets, and broke or removed every weapon they could find.

Ten men per company to bury the dead, was the order issued to each regiment on the morning of the 21st September; and a huge mound, composed of fifteen or sixteen gigantic graves, at the distance of about five hundred yards from the river, now marks the last resting-place of those who fell in the battle or died of their wounds in the ambulances.

Marshal St. Arnaud proposed an immediate advance of the entire army; but the humane Lord Raglan declined to leave the scene of action until the wounded were attended to; and when at length, on the 22nd, the allied armies broke up from their melancholy bivouac among the graves of their comrades, and set out on their chosen march with no fixed aim or project, the Russian wounded still lay in hundreds on the ground.

Then was shown that noble humanity which is as genuinely British as high heroism. Dr. Thompson, of the 44th Regiment, with one attendant - John Macgrath, an Irish soldier of that corps - volunteered to remain on the field, where lay "the grey acre" of Russian wounded, 750 of whom had been lying in their blood for upwards of sixty hours. A flag of truce was his only and frail dependence for protection from the vindictive fury of the Cossacks who hovered on the heights that overlooked the scene of slaughter.

In his efforts to dress the wounds and relieve the sufferings of these men, Dr. Thompson toiled without ceasing, and afterwards, at many risks, rejoined his regiment at Balaclava, only to perish of cholera a few days after his return.

BALACLAVA, 1854,
CHARGE OF THE HEAVY BRIGADE

It was during the war in the Crimea that the general introduction of rifled small arms made the use of rifled cannon necessary, in order that artillery might remain, as before, the principal arm on the field of battle; and the year 1855 saw the Armstrong gun first tried in the School of Gunnery at Shoeburyness; and since then guns have gone on increasing so much in size, that now a single shot from a 35-ton (700-pounder) is equal to the whole broadside of a 74 of the days of Nelson. When writing of such enormous guns, "Heaven protect me," says M. Lacombe, "from yielding to any desire to prejudge this question; but involuntarily my mind goes back to the enormous bombards of the 14th century, and I cannot forget how short-lived was their existence." In the Crimea the elongated bullet was first used with the Minié rifle, but only to a limited extent. The gauge was about 16 - i.e., 16 bullets to the pound. The bullet had an iron cup fitted into a hollow in the base, in order to expand the lead in the grooves.

The Enfield rifle was an improvement on this firearm, and the Pritchet bullet was next used, with a conical hollow in the base, afterwards filled by a boxwood plug, and sometimes with one of compressed baked clay.

All the fire-arms used in the wars we have mentioned have now given place to the breechloader, which carries the art of gun-making a grand step in advance, beyond even the percussions of Andrew Forsyth, whose invention caused the abolition of the old flint musket. The Minié rifle was accepted as the regulation weapon of the French army in 1846; in 1857 they received rifled arms in lieu of the old smooth-bore muskets; and the Franco-Prussian war saw the Minié superseded in its turn by the Chassepot.

In the Crimea, as the wounds of our men proved, the Russians fired low; hence the majority of the gunshot wounds were in the lower extremities and in the middle of the body.

Soon after the Alma, there landed 5,000 marines, together with the heavy cavalry from Scutari, including the Scots Greys, whose Waterloo trophies on their appointments had caused a delay in their transmission, lest such might prove distasteful to our French allies.

The first great step in the new war had been won, and our troops marched hopefully onward, with the desire to crown their efforts by the capture of Sebastopol. Save at times a hovering Cossack or so, with his lance glittering in the sun, no enemy appeared to oppose their march. The cottages and villas they passed were deserted by the natives, who abandoned all they possessed to the mercy of the troops. Lord Raglan and his staff rode considerably ahead of the army, while the baggage train toiled slowly in the rear. Save the occasional presence of a cannon abandoned, and the hoof or wheel-tracks on the road, no trace remained of that host which but three days before had boasted that they would drive "the island curs - the red devils," for so they termed us, into the sea.

In the afternoon, the beautiful valley of Katcha was reached, and there, amid a fertile scene, the army halted. Not an inhabitant was to be seen. All had left the valley in fear of the invaders: and for the night the British occupied the village of Eskel.

On Sunday the 27th, the army was at the village of Belbek, where it was joined by the Scots Greys and the 57th, or West Middlesex Regiment. The French also received considerable reinforcements. A body of Russians was posted on the southern bank of the Belbek, but showed no intention of engaging the

Allies, who were now within four miles of Sebastopol, the green domes, white walls, and dark batteries of which were distinctly visible. As it was necessary to establish a communication with the fleets, on board of which were the battering train, the stores, and ammunition, the attention of the allied generals was turned to the pretty little harbour of Balaclava, seven miles south of the doomed city. An inlet of the Euxine, its harbour is almost land-locked, and was at one time so great a resort of pirates, that it was found necessary to stretch a chain across its mouth. It is commanded by an old Genoese fort, and in the year of Alma the town was composed of neat white houses, shaded by poplars, and inhabited by Arnouats.

It was decided to execute a flank movement, passing the head of the harbour of Sebastopol, and take possession of the place. It was necessary to communicate this intention to the fleets, which had followed the march of the allied armies, and the execution of this difficult service was undertaken by Lieutenant Maxse, a young naval officer, who, with great intrepidity, volunteered to ride alone, by night, through a wooded district, crowded by the irregular, and consequently more barbarous, troops of the enemy. This feat and service he performed in safety.

On the 25th our army was at Khutor Mackenzia, or Mackenzie's Farm, as our Scottish soldiers called it, and so named from one of the six Scottish admirals who had carried the Russian flag in the Black Sea, and the following day saw Balaclava in possession of the allied armies. The garrison was too feeble for serious resistance, and after a small show of opposition, yielded to superior numbers.

The landing of the siege-train then followed, and preparations for the investment of Sebastopol commenced in earnest. Many large ship-guns were sent on shore, together with 2,000 seamen, who lent most efficient aid in dragging the great ordnance over hilly ground that rises between Sebastopol and Balaclava. They were in the highest spirits at having to form a part of the land force, and they astonished the soldiers by their alacrity, jollity, and the ease with which they "tallyed on" to the drag-ropes, and trundled the enormous Lancaster guns to the front.

The ground occupied by the besieging armies was an elevated plateau, having the Euxine on the left, and protected by almost perpendicular cliffs of marble. Their right was posted on a range of lofty hills, which sloped abruptly into the Vale of the Tchernaya River; and a deep ravine intersected the green elevated ground, extending from the harbour of Sebastopol to Balaclava, and divided the camp into two parts. The British army took its ground to the right of the position, having its flank defended by the hills towards the open country, and commanding the road to the captured harbour. The left towards the sea was occupied by the French, who had established a communication with their own fleet at the bays on the north-western shore of the promontory.

The allied armies thus occupied a semi-circle, commanding the south side of the city and fortress, and possessing the heights that overlooked them. It was confidently supposed that Sebastopol would fall in a few days, though its northern side was conveniently left open, so that supplies and supports could, without end, be poured into it. The trenches and batteries were immediately commenced, and from each regiment strong working parties were detailed for this dangerous service.

Meanwhile, the Russians were not idle in the work of defence. With wonderful rapidity, enormous earthworks and bastions were erected, and by the time the attacking forces were in readiness to open fire, the town was strongly fortified on the threatened side; and as the plan of the besiegers comprehended an attack by sea, Prince Menschikoff adopted the desperate resolution of sinking six large line-of-battle ships at the mouth of the harbour. These effectually prevented the ingress of the hostile fleets, while their cannon and crews were added to the defence of Sebastopol.

At half-past six a.m., on the 17th of October, the bombardment began, and no power of description could portray the scene that ensued. The earth seemed to vibrate and shake beneath the roar of the gigantic ordnance, as the whole line of attack opened fire simultaneously. By a preconcerted plan, each battery was opposed to a certain antagonist. The Lancaster guns attacked the Round Tower, and its earthworks were assailed by a six and a two-gun battery on one side of the Crown Battery.

The French fired upon every ship in the harbour that was within range, and were severely engaged with a defence known as the Flagstaff Battery. For two hours dense volumes of smoke veiled the whole place; its domes and spires, its forts and harbours, were quite hidden from view. A breeze from the sea stirred the hitherto still air, and lifted the curtain of vapour. Then it became visible that the Round Tower had been severely mauled. At nine o'clock, a skillfully-directed Russian shell fell into one of the French magazines. The explosion was terrific; several guns were dismounted, a hundred artillerymen were destroyed, and the bodies of many were seen high in the air. Another explosion followed, and the French guns were silenced for that day.

The British guns did tremendous execution, and dismounted many of those of the enemy near the wall of the Redan; yet so persistent was the resistance, that our works were severely injured, and many of our men were killed or wounded; and the explosion of a powder-wagon was hailed by the Russians with hoarse and exulting shouts.

About noon, the allied fleets began to share in the operations. To the joy of the sailors, an order had been given on the previous day to clear away for action, and by nine a.m. the vessels drew near the scene of it. The sailing-vessels had each a small steamer to tow them; but the screw-steamers were independent of such aid. The French ships took up their position on the right of the entrance to the harbour, engaging the enormous gun tiers of Fort Quarantine and the other batteries on the southern side; while Sir Edward Lyons, in the Agamemnon of 90 guns, turned his broadside against Fort Constantine, and the remaining vessels formed a line across the inlet, and once more the roar of cannon seemed to shake the earth and sea. The naval attack raged till the descending night put an end to the cannonade, when, after suffering most serious loss, and exhibiting the most resolute courage, the fleets drew out of range. Our ships were greatly damaged, and it was felt that the effect their guns had produced on the casemated granite works of the enemy, was by no means equal to, or commensurate with, the injuries we had sustained.

The Albion, of 90 guns, and the Arethusa, of 50 guns, was completely crippled. The Retribution, of 28 guns, had her mainmast shot away, the Firebrand had scarcely a whole spar left, and the Triton was dreadfully mauled aloft, and received some shot in her paddle-wheels; but all the events of the siege, for the eight days after the opening of the fire on Sebastopol, though attended by a dreadful loss of life and limb, were insignificant when compared to those which occurred on the morning of the 25th of October, the anniversary of Agincourt, when -

"Half a league, half a league,
    Half a league onward,
All in the Valley of Death
    Rode the Six Hundred!"

In Colonel Denison's work on "Modern Cavalry," he says tritely, "Cavalry must never surrender - this is one of the established maxims of the arm, at any rate in a country that is all open; it must always attempt to cut its way through, or if that be impossible, by scattering to elude pursuit The charge of cavalry must be rapid and unexpected; it must be made with confidence and pushed home. There should be no doubt when the order to charge is once given, then caution should give place to impetuosity."

Some of these ideas were fully carried out at the battle of Balaclava, when the Death Ride bore glorious witness to the high-souled devotion, the discipline and splendid valour of the British cavalry, in whose annals it can never be forgotten.

We have stated the importance of the post of Balaclava to the Allies, hence the Russians made strenuous efforts to cut off the communication of the besiegers with that town, where their supplies were landed. On the other hand, the Allies left nothing undone to provide for its safety. Sir Colin Campbell had been appointed governor of Balaclava, and his garrison consisted of Highlanders, a body of marines from the fleet, while another body of 4,000 Turks, on the proper left of the position, commanded

Entrance to Balaclava Harbour

the road to the camp. One slender cavalry division, led by Lord Lucan, and composed of the Scots Greys, the Enniskillens, and 1st Royal Dragoons; the 4th and 5th Dragoon Guards forming the Heavy Brigade, under Brigadier Sir James Yorke Scarlett; with the 4th and 13th Light Dragoons, the 8th and nth Hussars, and the 17th Lancers, forming the Light Brigade, under Lord Cardigan, were between the Turkish redoubts and the 93rd Highlanders, who were encamped under some cliffs, on the summit of which the Royal Marines had thrown up batteries.

At seven in the morning of the 25th October, tidings came to head-quarters that a strong force of Russian cavalry, supported by infantry and artillery, had suddenly appeared in the valley below Balaclava, and attacked the Turkish redoubts, which they were taking in succession. The British 1st and 4th Divisions immediately got under arms, and began their march for the scene of action, while General Canrobert ordered General Bosquet, with 200 Chasseurs d'Afrique, and a force of artillery, to their assistance.

Sir Colin Campbell had promptly got the Sutherland Highlanders under arms. The shrill trumpets sounded "Boot and saddle!" among the tents and impromptu stables of the cavalry camp, and Lord Lucan's division were speedily mounted, with pistols and carbines loaded. The surface of the valley into which his two slender brigades advanced was very undulating, and the rounded waves of green land or grassy hillocks served for a time to conceal the movements of the different bodies of troops from each other. Above these hillocks could be seen the white smoke of the distant conflict curling, as the Russians stormed the four redoubts in quick succession, turning the guns of each, as they captured it, on the fugitive Turks, who fled in four great masses - decimated by round and grape shot from their own cannon, which, in their coward haste to escape, they had forgotten to spike - like sheep, towards the calm, steady line of the 93rd

Highlanders, on whose left flank Sir Colin formed them up in a confused body. While waiting the movements of the enemy, now 25,000 strong, he deemed it necessary to impress his Highlanders with the gravity of the occasion. He rode down the line, and said, -

"Remember, there is no retreat, men! You must die where you stand!" And the men replied, -

"Ay, ay, Sir Colin, we'll do that."

In fierce pursuit came on the Russian horse, with their polished lance-heads and glazed-leather helmets flashing in the morning sun. Squadron after squadron came in view, like the successive waves of a human sea. Reining up for a moment on die crest of the last line of hillocks, they seemed to look with wonder - it might be, perhaps, with something of contempt - on the thin red line of Scotsmen, whom, as Sir Colin said in his

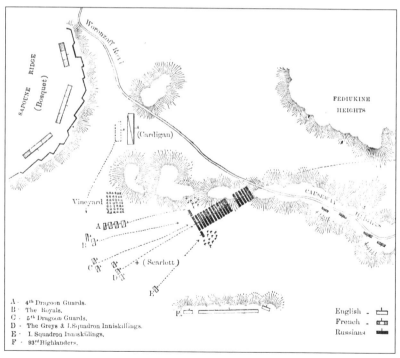

A · 4ᵗʰ Dragoon Guards.
B · The Royals.
C · 5ᵗʰ Dragoon Guards.
D · The Greys & I.Squadron Inniskillings.
E · I. Squadron Inniskillings.
F · 93ʳᵈ Highlanders.

English ·
French ·
Russians ·

The Heavy Cavalry Charge at Balaclava

quaint way, "he did not think it worth while to form four deep or in square." The regiment numbered only 550 men.

On with uplifted swords, or lances leveled, spurring came the Russians, with a sound as of thunder rolling through the air. This proved too much for the Assakiri Mansurei Mohamediyes, or "victorious soldiers of Mohammed," as they boasted themselves to be, and once more their line of red breeches was turned to the enemy, as they fled en masse, shouting "Ship, ship, ship!" while the solitary Highland regiment alone confronted the enemy, and hence came the brief telegram, which caused so much delight at home - "The Turks fled but the Scots stood firm."

The Sutherland Highlanders were drawn up on rising ground, in front of the village of Kadikoi, which they playfully named Dunrobin.

The word of command was heard; the Minié rifles were levelled from the shoulder; the black-plumed bonnets were seen to droop a little to the right and front, as each man took his steady aim; then from flank to flank a withering volley rang, and when the smoke rolled away, a confused heap of men and horses were seen writhing and tumbling over each other, with swords, lances, and caps scattered far and near. Many lay there who would rise no more, and beyond them all were seen the retreating squadrons - retreating as fast as they had come on.

Many other regiments - cuirassiers and lancers - joined the routed horse, as they re-formed on the slope of a hill, where they could see the light and heavy brigades of British cavalry drawn up in a small valley - the future "Valley of Death" - a little to the left of the Highlanders, and having had enough of them, they now seemed disposed to have a trial of strength with our troopers.

The fight was about to assume the character of a terrible tournament - a cavalry combat in open space, but between forces most unequal in numerical strength. Lord Raglan, with his staff, and the French generals, with theirs, had by this time reached the place of action, and from the lofty hills above the valley watched the scene that ensued. Not a word was spoken, scarcely a breath seemed to be drawn, so intense was the excitement, for by many thousands they outnumbered our small force of cavalry. Scarlett's Heavy Brigade mustered only 300 swords.

The Russian horse once more came on; but now they were formed in two long and compact lines.

The Scots Greys and the Enniskillens were the two advanced regiments of the Heavy Brigade, and instead of waiting to receive the charge; they gallantly rode forward to meet it. Side by side these two corps, which have ever fraternised in quarters, and have ridden together in every battle, from the plains of Minden to those of Waterloo, one in heart, in ardour, and in purpose, they went on, till at last their horses were at racing speed. As the adverse lines drew near, the Russians extended their overlapping flanks, as if to swallow the two regiments up. "Bending a little to the left the Scots met the Russian right, and the Enniskillens similarly engaged the advancing wing of the enemy's left. The shock was appalling."

The Greys, says Kinglake, gave no utterance save "a low, eager, fierce moan of rapture - the moan of outbursting desire. The Enniskillens went in with a cheer."

A ray of light seemed to pass along the squadrons, as the sword-blades flashed downward in the sunshine; then came the crash of battle. A loud cheer burst from the ranks of the Light Brigade, and from all who were looking on, and then for a few moments all was a wild chaos of mingled uniforms - scarlet, green, blue, and grey - of flashing swords and bannered lances, of helmets and standards, of shrieking men and snorting horses, and many an episode of chivalry, and many a hand-to-hand combat was there.

Overlapped by the vast extent of the first Russian line, it

was thought that the two regiments were lost forever, but by degrees they were seen to emerge from the chaos, and to be riding to attack the second line, after cutting a passage through the first. A sergeant of the 1st Dragoons states that they saw "one squadron of the Greys upset a whole regiment of them," and being conspicuous by their colour, on returning, many of their horses were covered with blood.

"We charged," says a Scots Grey, in his published letter - "Oh, God! I cannot describe it. They were so superior to us in numbers, and we were in the middle of them. I never certainly felt less fear in my life, and I hope God will forgive me, but I felt more like a devil than a man. We fought our way out of them, as only Britons can fight The 4th, 5th, and 6th were there up with us. I escaped without a scratch, though I was covered with blood. We cut them down like sheep, and the plain is covered with dead."

"Such cutting and slashing for about a minute was dreadful to see," says an English trooper of the 5th Dragoons, in writing to his parents; "the rally sounded, but it was no use, none of us would come away till the enemy retreated, then our fellows cheered as loudly as they could. When we were in the midst of them my horse was shot; he, fell and got up again, but I was entangled in the saddle, my head and one leg on the ground. He tried to gallop on with the rest, but fell again, when I managed to get loose. While I was in that predicament, a Russian lancer was about to run me through, but Macnamara came up at the time, and nearly severed his head from his body; so, thank God! I did not get a scratch."

When the tall black bearskins of the Scots Greys on the left, and the brass helmets of the Enniskillens on the right, began to re-appear, as they closed in and cut through the second Russian line, the remaining regiments of the Heavy Brigade, each of which in strength was little more than a squadron, dashed upon the disordered ranks of the first, and in less than five minutes the whole of this mass of Russian cavalry were flying rearward before the swords of our gallant "heavies."

Then the hushed silence which had sealed the lips of the spectators of this terrible but glorious scene (in which we had many wounded, but only five killed outright) was broken, and over the hills of Balaclava there rang such a cheer as can alone be raised by British soldiers or by British sailors flushed with victory.

Flying before these charges, which Sir James Scarlett led in person, the Russians, cavalry and infantry alike, retired into a narrow gorge at the head of the long green valley.

There, thirty pieces of cannon were placed in position, and six solid columns of cavalry and six of infantry were formed in rear of them, while other dense masses darkened all the slopes beyond.

To illustrate the emotions of some of our men on this most eventful day, we cannot do better than quote one or two of their letters which appeared in prints of the time.

"Dear father and mother," wrote a corporal of the 5th Dragoon Guards to his parents, "I am glad to tell you that we had an engagement with the Russians on the twenty-fifth of this month. We turn out in marching order every morning at four o'clock; it is quite dark then, so we stand to our horses till about one hour after daylight, because we expected an attack before this, as they have been gathering their army about three miles from our camp during the past fortnight.

"Well, on the morning of the twenty-fifth, just as daylight was breaking, the cannon commenced firing from our batteries on the hills, and at seven o'clock we advanced just opposite them.

We could not see our enemies, but they kept firing at our artillery, and shells were flying over our heads and dropping all around us. Our artillery had to retire, as they had no more ammunition; so after a while the Turks started, left the batteries, and ran down the hill as hard as ever they could. So the enemy got possession, and we could see them bringing their guns up the hill, and in a few minutes the shot and shell were coming pretty fast; they were firing six-pounders at us, and we could see the balls coming. We shouted, "Look out, boys! "They came with such force against the ground, that they would rise and go for half a mile before they touched the ground again. We and the Scots Greys lost some horses here, and had to retire out of range of the guns. We had no infantry up at the time, except the Highlanders, for the Turks had all run away, so the Russians came galloping over the hills.

"Some of them went to attack the Highlanders, who popped them off nicely, so they retired. In the meantime, another lot of cavalry came to attack us. I suppose they thought we should run. We wheeled into line, the 'charge' sounded! and away we went into the midst of them."

After relating that he was dismounted in the melee, the writer continues: - " I got up and ran to where I saw a lot of loose horses. I got one belonging to the Enniskillens, and was soon with the regiment again. When I first mounted, I saw a Russian who had strayed from the rest; he rode up and tried to stop me. As it happened, I had observed a pistol in the holster-pipe, so I took it out, and shot him in the arm; he dropped his sword. I then rode up and run him through the body, and the poor fellow dropped to the ground. Lord Lucan said, when we charged, that ' we were into them, and the devil would not get us away from them!' Lord Raglan sent his compliments to General Scarlett, and said that the Heavy Brigade behaved gallantly. We had only two men killed and fourteen wounded. In the evening they gave the Light Division a chance, and sent them to retake the guns. The poor fellows went, and not the half of them came back."

"You say you hear nothing of our regiment? "wrote another dragoon. "Well, I will tell you something about it now. In the first place, when coming from Varna across the Black Sea, we were overtaken by a most awful gale of wind. Our vessel, the Wilson Kennedy, went on her beam-ends, and the stabling gave way, all the horses were thrown over to one side of the ship, and in one horrid night more than a hundred of them kicked and worried each other to death: and there we were for two nights and days fastened down with the dead and dying horses.

"We only saved eleven out of our ship, and on the third day we threw a hundred and one overboard. We were eight days beating about the Black Sea, and had to go back to Constantinople, at which place they put us on board a steamer which landed us in the Crimea, and now indeed our work has begun!

"We are protecting the rear, while the besiegers are attacking the town. The whole of the cavalry are encamped on an open plain surrounded by hills, and we have indeed plenty cut out for us. Over these hills are thousands of Cossacks and a large Russian army trying to get up to Sebastopol, so it is our duty to keep them back. They are constantly coming down upon us, and we have had some severe struggles, but they have not the ' pluck ' of Englishmen.

"We are in the saddle night and day. I cannot tell how long it is since I was undressed. I only know it has been so long that I have forgotten it. The worst affair we have had was the day before yesterday.

"At dawn the enemy advanced in such numbers, that they took from the Turks two of their batteries, and turned the guns upon us, so we were obliged to retreat out of range. This so elated the enemy that they actually had courage enough to come into the open field against us. Three regiments of their cavalry then tried to gain the 93rd Highlanders' position, and charged them, but they had not time to repent, for they were cut down like corn, and what were left of them turned and fled, and we pursued them over the hills, where they were reinforced by three more regiments of cavalry, including Nicholas's crack Imperial Guards."

After describing the charge, in which he escaped unhurt, the writer, though liable to make some of those mistakes so common to one whose position was so subordinate, adds, "The plain is covered with dead Russians, and, of course, we left some of our poor comrades in the field. Well, when we had finished this lot, we thought of going home to breakfast. But no; they (the enemy) had some guns over the hills that Lord Raglan sent word were to be charged and captured at any cost.

"So off we went again, Lord Lucan leading the heavies and Lord Cardigan the Light Brigade. The latter charged first this time, took the guns, cut down the gunners, and then, when they thought all was right, they were met by thousands of Cossacks who had been in ambush. The Royals, the Greys, the 4th, 5th, and 6th now charged again!

"The butchering was repeated. I cannot describe to you the scene that ensued. The men on the right and left of me were both killed on the spot. We hacked our way out of it as well as we could, but were obliged to leave the guns. Colonel Yorke had his leg broken, and all the officers in the front rank were wounded."

In writing of the charge of the Heavy Brigade, a captain of the Enniskillen Dragoons says: -

"Twice I was unhorsed, and more than once had to grip my sword tighter, the blood streaming down over the hilt, and running up my very sleeve! Our old Waterloo comrades, the Greys, and ourselves, were the only fellows who first flung ourselves into the very heart of the Muscovites. Now we were lost in their ranks - anon in little bands battling - now in good order together - now in and out, until the whole heavies on the spot plunged into a forming body of the enemy, and helped us to end the fight, by compelling the foe to fly; but all this you have read in the papers.

"I cannot depict my feelings when we returned. I sat down completely exhausted, and unable to eat, though deadly hungry. All my uniform, my hands, and my very face, were bespattered with blood; but it was that of the enemy! But my mind was full of that exultation which it is impossible to describe."

" Dear mother," wrote one of the 4th Dragoons, "don't alarm yourself about me; I have a good hope I shall see you again; but I shall never forget the 25th of October. Shells, bullets, cannon-balls, and swords kept flying round us. I escaped them all, except a slight scar from the bursting of a shell; but, God be thanked, it did not disable me. Dear mother, every time I think of my poor comrades my blood runs cold. We had to gallop over the wounded."

When the Heavy Brigade had completed its rally, Sir Colin Campbell galloped up and spoke to the Greys. "Gallant Greys," said he, "I am sixty-one years old; but if I were young again, I should be proud to be in your ranks."

But now came the great disaster of an otherwise glorious day - the daring and romantic charge of the Light Brigade against the most overwhelming odds that were ever met in any battle in modern times - a charge that resulted in the almost entire destruction of the splendid regiments of our light cavalry, the hussars and lancers, &c, under the Earl of Cardigan. Nor has any such charge occurred in ancient times, unless we except the sally made from the castle of Alcoar by the hundred Christian knights led by Ruy Diaz, the Cid Campeador.

- C H A P T E R   V -

BALACLAVA, 1854,
CHARGE OF "THE SIX HUNDRED"

Notwithstanding the formidable array in the valley, in a position that was almost unassailable, a message was received by Lord Lucan, from Captain Lewis Edward Nolan, of the 15th Hussars - undoubtedly one of the bravest of the brave - to the effect that the Light Brigade was to carry the thirty pieces of cannon in front of the Russians. Another account - for this order was the cause of much subsequent disputation and speculation - says that he simply pointed with his sword towards the cannon, while saying, "We should take them," and that the action was mistaken for an order. Wherever the mistake lay, poor Nolan was fated soon to pay for the misconception with his life."

Lord Cardigan would seem to have tacitly acquiesced in what he deemed an order from Lord Raglan, and turning quietly in the saddle, said, "The brigade will advance!"

On this day he wore the uniform of his old regiment, the nth Hussars; but, instead of dangling from his left shoulder, his pelisse, richly covered with lace, was put on like a coat; yet it did not break the rigid outline of his fine figure. He rode a thoroughbred chestnut, and looked every inch a hussar. In this mode all our hussars in the Crimea wore their pelisses.

In succession each officer took up the words, "The brigade will advance. First squadron - marches - trot - gallop!"

It did not amount to the strength of one good regiment, as it mustered only 673 of all ranks in that eventful hour, when, sweeping over the grassy ground towards where the green-painted Russian artillery stood with gaping muzzles, before the solid wall of five and twenty thousand horse and foot - those dark columns in dull grey or clay-coloured capotes, with belts crossed and bayonets fixed, and the darker-clad cavalry, whose lances and sword-blades glittered like a forest of steel in the sun.

On and on rode the Light Brigade; inspiring wonder in those they were to attack, while Cardigan led them on with brandished sword. Each trooper's hand was firm on his bridle, each grasp was firm on the sword, as, holster to holster, and boot to boot, the dragoons swept on, their horses with necks outstretched and manes streaming backward like smoke on the wind.

The moment they were within range of the Russian guns, the whole park of artillery shook the air like the thunder of heaven, while they, with shot, shell, grape, and rockets, and infantry with their tempest of conical rifle-bullets, from front and both flanks, tore through horses and men, and down went both on every side.

Bursting on the right front of Lord Cardigan, a Russian shell threw out a fragment which struck Captain Nolan, who had joined in the charge, full on the chest, and penetrated the heart. The sword fell from his hand, but the hand still remained uplifted high in air, and the grasp of the practised horseman still lingered on the bridle; but the horse wheeled about and began to gallop back upon the advancing brigade. "Then, from what had been Nolan," says Kinglake, "and his form was still erect in the saddle, his sword-arm still high in air, there burst forth a cry so strange and appalling, that the hussar who rode nearest him has always called it unearthly. And in truth I imagine the sound resulted from no human will, but rather from those spasmodic forces which may act upon the form when life has ceased. The firm-seated rider, with arm uplifted and stiff, could hardly be ranked with the living. The shriek men heard rending the air was scarcely other than the shriek of a corpse!"

Vindicating even in death his reputation as one of England's noblest horsemen, he passed through an interval of the 13th Light Dragoons, and then dropped out of the saddle. Down - down - thick and fast, were going men and horses now, and shrieks and prayers, hurrahs and curses, rose upward together; but, filling the gaps, the flanks closed in, and firmer, wilder, denser, became the death-ride down the valley. Here and there

Captain Nolan

the troopers could no longer be restrained from darting in front of their officers, as the genuine English racing spirit broke out, each man striving to outride the other. Above the varied sounds and the rush of the troops, one voice rose clearly, - " Now, my brave lads, for old England! Conquer or die!"

The speaker was Lord George Paget, who rode at the head of the 4th Light Dragoons. He was a peer's son; but every man who rode there, even to the youngest trumpeter, was a knight as true as any that ever rode at Crecy or Flodden Field. In this headlong rush, the 17th Lancers were subjected to much of the "rending perturbance" created among cavalry by the sinking and wild plunging of every wounded horse, and again, by the piteous intrusion of it, riderless, in the midst of the battle, as it sought to wedge itself into its old troop. At one time there were four horses thus abreast of Lord George Paget, on one side, and five on the other, all with saddles empty, and all impelled by terror and the habit of ranging in line. On and on yet they rode. Many a familiar face had vanished now, and men who were on the flanks found themselves in the centre, and "familiar pulpit reflections concerning man's frail tenure of life came to have all the air of fresh truth, when pressed upon the attention by the ping of the bullet, the sighing and humming, and at last the 'whang' of the round-shot, by the harsh whirr of the jagged iron fragments thrown abroad from a bursting shell, by the sound most abhorred of all those heard in battle - the sound that issues from the moist plunge of the round shot when it buries itself, with a 'slosh', in the trunk of a man or horse."

On and on yet, like a whirlwind, swept our gallant Light Brigade - the flower of the three kingdoms, all well trained and nobly mounted, the hearty British "Hurrah! Hurrah!" ringing high in the air, and soon the red flashing muzzles of the guns were passed; the gunners were casting themselves beneath the wheels and limbers to escape the cut of sword and thrust of

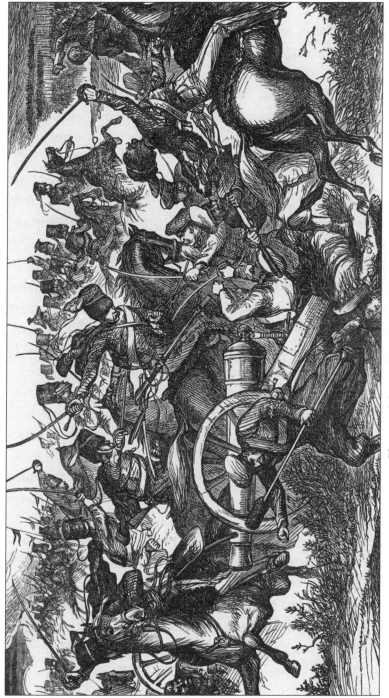

Charge of the Light Cavalry at Balaclava

lance; others were rushing for shelter to the squares of infantry, whose musketry rained now a ceaseless shower of lead. The guns were taken, their gunners swept away, and next the Russian cavalry were attacked and a literal forest of Cossack lances and cuirassier swords, was hewn at through and through, but the survivors of the charge were breathless, their horses blown, and when reining up, they found themselves without being supported effectually.

"It's all up - threes about - retire!" was now the order, and back again, but rearward now, exposed once more to a murderous fire, rode all that remained of the 673 men of the Light Brigade. It was reduced to a mounted strength of only 195. Of the 13th Light Dragoons, only ten men remained in the saddle, out of 112 who had paraded; of the 17th Lancers, there remained but thirty-four, and when the melancholy roll was gone over again, it was found 113 had been killed, 134 wounded; and that, including 43 horses shot as unserviceable, the brigade had 475 horses killed besides having forty-two wounded.

A sergeant of the 17th Lancers writes: "There were not many men in the 17th who did not receive some injury, lost their horses, had them wounded or had some part of their appointments carried away by shot or shell. I had my lance broken close to my knee." Captain Morris, who led the corps, was severely wounded in the head, and Sir William Gordon was covered with lance and sabre wounds. Major Clarke, of the 5th Dragoon Guards, rode into Balaclava with his helmet gone, his head bound up, and so covered with blood that none could recognise him; and the surgeons at work on the wounded, with their sleeves turned up, were so splashed and bespattered, that they looked more like butchers than medical men, yet the wounded exulted when the cheers of those were heard who went in for completing the task they had begun, and for avenging them, under Paget and Shewell; and when, from before 230 Britons, the bulk of that powerful Russian cavalry, which numbered itself by thousands, was falling back. This result was strange; but it was produced by the moral effect of the recent charge upon the mind of the Russian troops.

Kinglake relates, that when the remnant of "the Six Hundred" had formed up, Lord Cardigan came forward and said -

"Men! It is a mad-brained trick, but no fault of mine."

"Never mind, my lord," answered some of them, "we are ready to go in again."

"No, no, men!" said he, "you have done enough."

But when the earl made his report to Lord Raglan, the latter said angrily, -

"What did you mean, sir, by attacking a battery in front, contrary to all the usages of war?"

"My lord," replied the earl, "I hope you will not blame me, for I received the order to attack from my superior officer."

And subsequently Lord Raglan not only determined that the justification thus offered was sound, but also, it seems, formed an opinion that Lord Cardigan's whole conduct in the affair had been admirable.

Lord Cardigan received a lance-thrust through his uniform in this charge. Our men were mostly slain by this weapon - one fine young English dragoon was found lying dead, with no less than thirteen lance-wounds in his body. Another of the 17th had six such thrusts in his body, and two horses killed under him; he received five bullets in his saddle, one or two through his cap, and one in the shaft of his lance.

Such was the result of this desperate cavalry charge. "It is, we believe, almost impossible," says a writer, "to find a greater instance of discipline and devotion to duty, of more romantic courage or desperate adventure. It showed us that the British heart was as high in spirit, and the British arm as strong as in the knightly days of old."

In hot temper Lord Cardigan came back from the charge, and, meeting General Scarlett, exclaimed -

"What do you think of the aide-de-camp who brought us the order which has destroyed the Light Brigade - riding to rear, screaming like a woman?"

"Do not say any more," replied Sir James Scarlett; "I have just ridden over his body."

When the earl spoke he was ignorant of Nolan's fate, and the singular mode of his death.

So reduced was our cavalry force by these operations, that when there was a review on the Queen's birthday, before Sebastopol, five regiments could muster only 387 mounted men.

At Balaclava, says a writer, the Earl of Cardigan fought like a Paladin of old, and his officers and men were indeed worthy of such a chief. Lord George Paget fought at the head of his regiment, and proved himself a worthy son of 'the old Marquis of Anglesey, of Peninsular and of Waterloo renown.

INKERMAN, 1854

Though the Russians had been so unsuccessful hitherto, they neither lost heart, nor were likely to yield without a desperate struggle. The steady bravery of the Allies had now impressed upon the Emperor Nicholas the necessity for sending large reinforcements to the Crimea, and with them came his two sons, the Grand Dukes Michael and Nicholas. All troops available at Odessa were forwarded through the Isthmus of Perekop, of which the Allies did not possess themselves; and they were conveyed in every species of vehicle that they might arrive at the scene of operations fresh thus the first week of November saw fully 50,000 additional troops brought into Sebastopol, one side of which was uninvested. To General Osten-Sacken and other officers of rank one of the Grand Dukes held out threats of degradation and Siberia, if the Allies were not attacked and the siege raised.

The Russian plan was evidently to make a grand attack on the right of the British lines, and occupy them effectually, while a simultaneous assault from the city should be made on those of the French, who, it was naturally supposed, would detach a large portion of their army to our assistance. The plan of the great sortie was admirably schemed; six of the most experienced generals in Russia were to take part in it, and so great was the number of their troops, that there seemed every probability of their hurling the invaders into the Euxine.

On the morning of Sunday, the 5th of November, the grand attempt was to be made.

On the evening of Saturday, the 4th, the Bishop of Sebastopol preached to the soldiers, assuring them that the blessings of heaven and of all the saints of holy Russia would be upon their enterprise - that crowns of martyrdom awaited all who fell. "The island curs," they were told, were monsters of cruelty, who tortured and committed the most unheard-of barbarities upon all captives who fell into their relentless hands. They were abominable and bloodthirsty heretics, whose extermination was the solemn duty of all who wished to serve God and their father the Emperor. He further assured them the British camp teemed with immense treasure, golden vessels and sacks of precious stones, the spoil of ravaged India: and of these pretended treasures, one-third would become the property of the victors. After their religious rancour, their nationality, and their avarice had been thus duly inflamed, the generals ordered large quantities of the coarse ardent spirit called raki to be freely distributed, and thus, half intoxicated and wholly excited, they clamoured to be led to battle.

All the bells in Sebastopol rang a tocsin while the troops composing the sortie, at the early hour of 3 a.m., stole forth under favour of the darkness and a dense mist, and entered the ravines near the Tchernaya, which were near the British right, and our weakest point. These movements were unknown to our outpickets, and unheard by them, though more than one wary old soldier asserted that he heard "something like the rumble of artillery wheels," during the very time that the hills commanding the position were being occupied by several large guns. Cautiously and noiselessly the Russian troops stole on, their footsteps hidden by the clanging of the great bells, till 50,000 of them were on the flank as well as in front of our lines, and the first intimation the pickets had of their presence in that unexpected quarter, was finding themselves almost surrounded by an overwhelming force.

Knapsacks were generally thrown aside, but the muskets of the outlying pickets were in some instances so wet from exposure overnight, that they failed to explode. The firing speedily came fast and furious now on every side, and as the main body of the army got in all haste under arms, the musketry - flashing like red streaks through the grey gloom towards the head of the beautiful valley of Inkerman - warned all of a resolute sortie.

Fighting desperately, the pickets retreated to a small redoubt, or 2-gun battery, which had been erected at that point by the suggestion of Sir De Lacy Evans, but which, from our reduced numbers, and the large extent of ground we were compelled to occupy, had been dismantled; and now it was rapidly destined to become the scene of one of the bloodiest conflicts in history. The Russian artillery now opened fire from the slopes of those hills which they had reached unseen; at the same moment, all the batteries of the town, as if further to distract the Allies from the real point of attack, opened a simultaneous cannonade, which dashed to pieces the huts of our men, tore up their tents, and did dreadful execution in their ranks.

The brave fellows of our 55th, or Westmoreland Regiment, peppered the advancing foe through the grass-grown embrasures of the small redoubt; but a rapid charge was made to drive them from their slender position. Nobly and resolutely did this small body of Britons withstand the human flood of inflamed and furious Muscovites that surged around them - a column mustering forty men to one - till at length, compelled to fall back, leaving their merciless foes in the redoubt, in which they bayoneted or brained the wounded. Into their thin ranks, as day dawned, the batteries on the hills poured down their iron tempest, and not a man of that regiment would have been left alive to tell its story, had not the 41st Welsh and the 49th Hertfordshire now come into action.

Forming line, these two corps advanced against the enemy, who, as a writer says, had that peculiar quality of race "which is superior to the common fighting courage possessed indiscriminately by all classes - the passive, concentrated firmness which can take every advantage, so long as a chance is left, and die without a word at last, when hope gives place to the sullen resignation of despair."

The scene of this conflict, though partly hidden by the mist, with which the smoke of the fire-arms mingled, is both beautiful and picturesque. In the foreground, a quaint old bridge spanned the Tchernaya, which winds from the lovely Baidar Valley through the most luxuriant verdure, and flows into the harbour of the beleaguered city, between precipitous white cliffs, which are literally honeycombed with cells and chapels. Thus, says Oliphant, in his "Shores of the Black Sea," Inkerman is well named the "City of the Caverns," and the remains, which exist there, tell of races long since departed, and of those constructions which display all the perseverance and ingenuity of more modern times. They are supposed to have been hollowed out by Greek monks during the reigns of the emperors of the Middle Ages, and when the Arians were persecuted in the Chersonesus, many of them found safety in these almost inaccessible abodes. There, too, are found empty sarcophagi of stone in the cells, which are connected with each other by stairs cut in the solid rock, and of these stairs and holes the skirmishers were not slow to avail themselves as places from whence to take quiet "pot-shots."

Above all these caverns tower the ivied ruins of an ancient fort; but whether it was the Ctenos built by Diophantes to guard the Heraclean wall, or the Theodori of the Greeks, mattered little to our troops then, as they pressed forward beneath its shadow to close with the enemy. In this quarter there were but 12,000 British troops in all to oppose the mighty hordes of General Osten-Sacken!

Forming line as they advanced, the Welsh and 49th Regiments

charged up the hill towards the redoubt, and attacked the enemy with brilliant gallantry. Storming they came, shoulder to shoulder, and hurled back the Russians, hundreds of whom - as they were massed in dense columns - fell before the deadly fire of the Minié rifle, and the desperate rush of the headlong bayonet charge that followed it. In the ranks of this and other regiments were many men fresh from Britain - men to whom the long grey-coated and spike-helmeted or flat-capped troops of the enemy among whom they now found themselves hand to hand and muzzle to muzzle, had been a species of myth, heard of only through the medium of the public prints, and now they had become a terrible reality.

Again, however, the batteries dealt destruction in the British ranks, and again they were compelled to fall back before the pressure of unwieldy numbers. The din of battle was growing louder, deeper, hoarser, in the valley, and our troops pressing onward to the attack, in many places could see only the flashing of the musketry in front, the tall brushwood and stunted oaks through which they had to move being in some places fully breast-high; thus some corps did not see the Russians until they were within pistol-shot of them.

The whole British army was in motion now. Lord Raglan and all the generals of division were in their saddles and upon the scene. Sir De Lacy Evans, who had retired ill on board of a ship, left his bed on the alarm being given, and, looking pale and worn, was present in the field. General Strangeways was soon able to bring an artillery force to bear upon the Russian guns, and ere long he silenced their destructive fire.

As our artillery came in upon the right, an officer of that force relates that "the Minié balls flew among them like hailstones- - an old simile, but not the less true;" that his mare was wounded in two places, and Major Townsend had his horse shot under him. Shot and shell next began to fall thick among the artillery, who were met by some of our infantry falling back. The crest of the hill was at that time covered with smoke, and the entire ground so encumbered by gorse and other bushes, that the guns were wheeled to the front with the greatest difficulty. Suddenly the curtain of smoke lifted, and within ten yards of the cannon were seen the ranks of the Russian infantry, with their long capotes and flat glazed caps, blazing away at our gunners, and mowing them down with ease. Major Townsend, who saw the critical position of his guns in that part of the field, gave the order at once to retire, as he was unsupported; but the order came too late, for the Russians were upon him.

Five pieces of cannon out of his six escaped, and one gunner coolly spiked it. On seeing it taken, Major Townsend turned his horse, and cried to Lieutenant Miller, the commander of the battery to which the gun belonged, "You won't disgrace me?" but the exclamation had scarcely left his lips when a shell burst amid the brigade, and a fragment dashed his head to pieces. Miller drew his sword, and, single-handed, galloped towards the captured gun, riding down one Russian and hewing down another. He alone routed a dozen of the enemy, and re-took the gun, without receiving the slightest wound.

In the other part of the field, where our artillery had better success, General Strangeways was by this time lying on the ground with his left leg smashed by a cannon-shot, and bleeding so profusely that he died on a stretcher soon after.

Another gallant effort to regain the redoubt was made by the 20th and 47th. Of the former slender corps, 200 men had just come in from the trenches, after twenty-four hours of exposure and rain; but the bugle called all to the front - 500 strong. Their orders were to support the Guards, who were heavily pressed by the enemy, many of whom crouched among the brushwood, but were driven down the hill. "We killed numbers of them," says an officer of the 20th (of old the regiment of Wolfe and

Kingsley), "and as we had no orders to halt, we continued keeping along the hill-side, about halfway down, and firing at the retreating enemy. I then heard the bugle sound to 'retire,' and set about trying to get the men back, no easy matter, as by this time, from several regiments being sent after each other, they were all mixed up."

After a few minutes' possession of the redoubt, the two regiments were forced to retire. But during these few minutes there was a frightful massacre on both sides. The ground about the work was literally heaped with dead; and again the Russians, on gaining possession of the redoubt, slaughtered all our wounded.

For a short time the battle had been confined chiefly to the artillery on the opposite hills, when the Guards advanced, under the Duke of Cambridge, and charging into the redoubt, retook it, ferreting the Russians out at the point of the bayonet; and the possession of it was retained by a few hundred of the Coldstreams against at least 6,000 of the enemy. Thrice, with hoarse shouts, the grey-coated masses, with all their bayonets glittering, hurled their valour and their strength madly and bravely up hill against the redoubt, and thrice they were hurled back with slaughter and defeat.

From Sebastopol fresh troops were every instant pouring to reinforce the sortie; and ere long the little band in the redoubt was surrounded by a wild horde of infuriated men - infuriated by the protracted conflict and the raki with which they had been supplied. Back to back the Coldstream Guardsmen fought, desperately, for their very lives. Their comrades were falling fast, and beneath their feet the ground was slippery with blood. Their pouches were emptying fast, as their ammunition became expended, and then they were compelled to hurl stones; and next, clubbing their muskets, they beat back the foe, obtained room to form line, and then, with levelled bayonets, they burst through the yielding mass, and, leaving more than a thousand Russian dead behind them, regained the Household Brigade.

While the Second and Light Divisions were engaging the enemy with undaunted bravery in front of our lines, Sir George Cathcart - a veteran Scottish officer, who had served as aide-de-camp to Lord Cathcart at Lutzen Boutzen, Dresden, and Leipzig, and afterwards at Quatre Bras and Waterloo - with the daring hardihood which distinguished him, led on his division, the 4th, in hope to relieve the Guards from the assault they were sustaining with such high valour. Uniting with his force the wreck of the Coldstreams, who re-formed under cover of his advance, he now found himself opposed to some 9,000 Russians. Undismayed by the disparity of force, this old soldier - who came of a warlike race, as he was the lineal descendant of that Alan Cathcart whose valour at Loudoun Hill was conspicuous in 1307 - gave the word for the 4th Division to advance, and, sword in hand, he was in the act of leading the charge, when a ball whistled through his heart, and he fell from his horse to rise no more.

So vast was the strength of the Russians that it was impossible so unequal a contest could continue, and, retiring slowly towards their lines, our gallant fellows disputed every foot of ground, and hundreds were falling hourly. The Russians picked off our officers - many of whom had gone into action in their full uniforms, while their men were in great coats - and when the former fell, bayoneted them on the ground, or dashed out their brains with the butt-ends of their muskets. The soldiers' letters, with which the prints of the time were full, teem with details of this Muscovite barbarity. The Duke of Cambridge was once quite surrounded, and had it not been for Dr. Wilson, of the 7th Hussars, drawing his sword and cheering a few men on, he must have been killed or taken: and by eleven o'clock in the forenoon the enemy were close to the tents of the 2nd Division.

Among the prisoners who fell into our hands was a Russian major, who had been heard more than once ordering his men to murder the wounded.

It was now that General Canrobert, with three regiments of Zouaves, five of Infantry of the Line, and a strong force of artillery, commenced a vigorous attack upon the Russian flanks, and then the issue of the fight did not long remain dubious; and most welcome to the ears of our men was the sound of the Zouave trumpets, and of the French drummers beating the pas de charge. The issue of the fight was no longer doubtful now. As at the Alma, a strange wail of despair came from many of the Russian regiments, as they wavered, broke, and tied towards the range of hills above Sebastopol, pursued hotly and trodden down by the mingled British and French soldiers.

By three o'clock they were totally routed, and we had obtained another complete victory, but at a terrible loss of life. The area of the field of battle was very limited and unvarying,

Sebastopol

being nearly confined to the Valley of Inkerman and the small works captured by and retaken from the enemy. The scenes on every side far transcended the horrors of a battle-field in general, and many of our dead were found, when cold and stiff, with hands uplifted, and horror and entreaty depicted in their white faces, showing that they had been murdered in cold blood, and had perished in the act of supplication.

A soldier of the 49th Regiment had a remarkable combat with some of those butcherly Muscovites when prostrate on the ground with a ball in his thigh. To protect himself, he had reloaded his musket, and picked up, luckily, a revolver which had been dropped by a wounded officer, at a time when four Russian soldiers and an officer came prowling through the bushes, assassinating the bleeding and helpless. Only one of these had his musket loaded, as the 49th man saw by his thumb being on the lock of his piece, so he instantly shot him. On this the other three drew near with their bayonets fixed. One he killed by hurling his musket at him, so that the bayonet lodged in his breast; the other two he wounded by the revolver, and compelled the officer to yield his sword. Snatching it afterwards from him, the Russian, little thinking there was another ball in the pistol, dealt the soldier a severe wound, and was instantly shot down.

Generals Cathcart, Strangeways, and Goldie, and Colonel Seymour, were among the slain. Generals Sir George Brown, Bentinck, Adams, and Torrens, with Colonel Gambier of the Artillery, were among the wounded. We had, altogether, 43 officers and 416 men killed; 103 officers and 1,849 men wounded; with 198 of all ranks missing. The Russian loss could not have been much under 14,000 men, including three of their generals.

Among their dead on that field lay the chief aide-de-camp of Prince Menschikoff, Woronzow Greig, son of Sir Alexis Greig, who commanded the Russian fleets at the sieges of Anapa and Varna, and grandson of the Scotsman, Samuel Greig, so well known as "the Father of the Russian Navy." But shortly before the battle he had been the bearer of a flag of truce to Lord Raglan.

For days the burial parties were engaged in interring the slain. Full honours were paid to the remains of Sir George Cathcart and the other generals who had fallen; and in one grave, side by side, were placed eleven officers of the Brigade of Guards. Some of these were very young men, and had displayed the most heroic courage.

This brilliant but terrible victory sent to the already overcrowded hospital at Scutari a frightful addition of wounded and dying men. Borne in the arms of their comrades from the field of battle, jolted in rude conveyances over the hills to Balaclava, they were embarked in small and filthy transports, to be tossed on the waves of the Euxine. In the passage across it many perished, amid the terrible deficiency of medical assistance, and even of medicine and dressings; each ship was veritably "a chaos of dying men, ghastly wounds, filth, cholera, and fever!"

Thousands of emaciated sufferers reached the shores of the Bosphorus, and were landed in open boats; those who were able to do so staggered or crawled, or weakly dragged their dying comrades to the doors of the hospital, where for such a sudden influx of patients there was no adequate accommodation. Many reached the doors, and sank never to rise again - some on the stairs, others in the passages; others clung more closely to life, and for days and days, lay upon the bare boards till the beds of the dead became vacant.

Writing of Inkerman, an army surgeon says: -

"Fighting is certainly most exciting work; but the result - how dreadful! and how sickening the contemplation of the battle-field, although there is even a fascination - if I may so

Charge of the Guards at Inkerman

speak - in it, which curiously disposes one to examine it, in all its dread details. There were to be seen hundreds of slain and wounded strewing the ground; in some places they were lying in heaps - British, French, and Russians - all slumbering in the friendship of death!

"On the day following the battle, after taking care that my own men were properly provided for, I volunteered my services to the wounded Russians, when, having selected many of the most urgent cases, I was employed from morn to eve in relieving, so far as lay in my power, the sad sufferings of the maimed. It would appear strange to be told that extensive surgical operations, after most serious wounds, afforded mitigation from pain; but so it is, for how tranquil are the sufferers at the moment they have lost their limbs under the surgeon's knife, in comparison to what they were, when lying unassisted and uncared for in their wounded condition!

"Very many of the poor fellows manifested the greatest gratitude for the services I rendered them, seizing my hands, and covering them 'with kisses, and by their upward looks implored the blessing of heaven on their benefactor. Alas!" continues this humane officer, "little do they know of the Englishman's heart, if they think he would do other than befriend those who are suffering, and whose miseries had been occasioned solely by him, when pursuing the stern dictates of duty."

Another medical officer (the surgeon of the Scots Fusilier Guards) mentions: -

"Some of the incidents that came under my notice were very appalling. A wounded man was being conveyed on a stretcher, carried on the shoulders of four others. When within a few yards of me, to my horror, a round shot levelled the whole group to the ground. Another ball, about the same time and locality, fell amongst a group of picketed horses, completely disembowelling one of them. The writhing's and agony of the poor animal were pitiable to witness. ...A ball - twenty-four-pounder - came through the tent on the side opposite to that where I was engaged, killing one of the orderlies assisting the surgeon, and also the pony of the latter, tied up a yard or two off."

After the Battle of Inkerman, Sebastopol was not assaulted, as many in the army fully expected it would be, at once. The 28th were coming from Malta; the 97th, or Earl of Ulster's, and the 99th, or Lanarkshire Regiment, and more French troops, were expected; but it soon became evident that the Allies were to winter before the blockaded city when the wood for the erection of huts began to arrive at Balaclava, and was slowly and laboriously brought to the front on Tartar ponies and the horses of the cavalry, who deemed their chargers degraded by such work. Already the soldiers were in rags; no two men were clad alike, and their uniforms were comically patched with clothing gleaned off the battle-field, and even with pieces of sacking and blanket.

When the new regiments landed, they marched in with the pomp of war, forming a strange contrast to the gaunt, bearded, and tattered men who welcomed them. But in a few short weeks the glitter was gone; their uniforms were as torn, worn, and daubed with the mud of the trenches, as those of the older Crimean men; and hunger, cold, cholera, and fever soon destroyed many ere they could cross their bayonets with the Russians.

The days and nights of duty in the trenches were simply horrible! The troops shivered there for twenty-four hours at a time, often amid mud that rose nearly to the knee, and, as the winter drew on, became frozen, especially towards the early and darker hours of the morning; and there they huddled together for warmth, watching the red bombs that whistled in a fiery arc overhead, or listening for the sounds that might indicate a Russian mine below.

The year 1855 saw the completion of the railway between Balaclava and the camp, and after that it was used for the conveyance of the sick and wounded to the hospitals; but only the wagons constructed for carrying the stores to the front were available for this important service, and they being unprovided with any contrivance to make them suitable for invalids, the more infirm, or more severely injured, could not be sent by them. So truly did the soldiers say that "John Bull liked glory - but liked to have it cheap."

This was the first time that any railway was employed for the transit of sick and wounded soldiers from the scene of actual hostilities to the rear, or that there was seen the strange spectacle of a locomotive screaming and puffing, to the field of war with biscuits, beef, and rum, arid stores of shot and Shell.

There was another novel feature in this Russian war quite unknown to the hero's of Vittoria and Waterloo.

An electric wire passed from the Crimea, under the Black Sea, to the shore of Bulgaria, and thence to Britain, whence every turn in the contest was thus known an hour or two after its occurrence.

CHAPTER VII

FINAL BOMBARDMENT OF SEBASTOPOL, 1855

Before the year closed, a smart affair, known as the capture of the "Ovens," took place on the night of the 20th of November, six days after the terrible hurricane which introduced most of the miseries our army had to endure. In the combat referred to, three companies of the 1st Battalion of the Rifle Brigade greatly distinguished themselves. The Russians had discovered a position in front of our advanced works (towards the left of the left attack), from whence they could greatly annoy the French working and covering parties. In some of the ancient caverns and old stone huts used by the Tartar shepherds during more peaceful times, they had securely ensconced themselves, and were thus enabled to keep up a heavy fire in security, at a distance of only two hundred yards.

This fire soon became intolerable, and 200 of our riflemen were ordered to dislodge them.

Dividing his force, Lieutenant Tryon advanced slowly with fifty of them from the body of the work, and crept silently and stealthily along the broken ground towards the enemy, who, surprised by the suddenness of the attack, scampered out of their holes and fled, while our men stumbled over many of them in their blankets, asleep and in the dark. Following in pursuit, the Rifles fixed their sword-bayonets, attacked the Russian supports under a sharp fire, and drove them away.

They then posted themselves in the very places occupied by the enemy - the caverns and old huts; and capturing all their blankets and great-coats, commenced to reverse the loop-holes for the reception of the Russians, who soon returned in two columns, which were only kept at bay by the sharp and deadly fire of the Rifles, whose ammunition, however, began to fall short.

Then the enemy came confidently on, and had to be repelled by the sword-bayonet. A third time they came on to the assault, but were again driven back, the supports of the Rifles having now come up with ammunition. For the remainder of the night the "Ovens" were held in peace, with heaps of Russian dead around them; but Lieutenant Tryon was mortally wounded by a bullet in the temple. In him the brigade lost one of its best officers - a brave and resolute soldier, who at Inkerman used his rifle with more deadly success and certainty than any of his men. He was interred on Cathcart's Hill, where now a simple slab marks his grave. The Rifles had only eight men killed and fifteen wounded in this affair, which drew praises from General Canrobert in his order of the day to the French army, adding: -

"Our Allies held firm, with their well-known energy, and remained masters of the place where we see them posted this morning. I wish to render homage before you to the vigour with which this coup de main was accomplished, and which has caused the death of the brave Lieutenant Tryon. We shall pay him the regret due to his glorious end. It will draw closer the bonds of fraternity in arms which unite us to our Allies.

"Canrobert.
"Head-quarters, Nov. 22nd."

And so, after this, the old year died out without any event of importance, amid an amount of sickness, wretchedness, and misery unknown in war since the retreat from Moscow.

On the 2nd of March 1855, the Emperor Nicholas, the originator of the war, died; but it still went on under his son

Alexander. An expedition to Kertch and the Sea of Azof, in May, destroyed many Russian ships and towns in that quarter. Sardinia having joined the British and French alliance, her troops, in conjunction with those of the latter, won a brilliant victory on the banks of the Tchernaya. And twice during the war the French and British leaders were changed; St. Arnaud, dying after the victory of the Alma, was succeeded by Canrobert, who in May 1855, gave place to General (afterwards Marshal) Pelissier. In June, the good, gallant, and gentle Lord Raglan died of cholera, and was succeeded in the command by Lieutenant-General Sir James Simpson, a Peninsular veteran, who had served at the siege of Cadiz, the attack on Seville, been wounded at Quatre Bras, and who had served as second in command under the fiery Sir Charles Napier, against the mountain and desert tribes on the right bank of the Indus, in 1845, and yet who, withal, lacked sufficient energy for the task assigned him.

In Connolly's "History of the Sappers and Miners," afterwards called the Royal Engineers, we have some graphic pictures of the difficult duties they performed before Sebastopol, and of the perilous risks they encountered in pressing the works of the siege.

In front of the batteries on the left attack there were commenced a number of rifle-pits, which subsequently became an extensive series of screens, spotting the ridge on its very brow, each connected with the other by an approach, which in time encircled the hill, and formed a continuous line of entrenchment for musketry fire, within fair range of the enemy's batteries and quarries. When the nights were clear, and the moon or starlight bright, a heavy cross-fire of shells and grape was constantly poured upon the Sappers and working-parties, rendering their operations alike perilous and trying; but this was well repaid by the security with which our riflemen from their pits or screens picked off the Russian gunners, and thus silenced some of the ordnance which cannonaded the trenches from the Redan and barrack batteries.

The Round Hill trench - an astonishing achievement of perseverance and skill, formed, for the most part, through rock, at an extraordinary outlay of labour and of life, under very adverse circumstances, and interruptions from the fire of artillery and of musketry - was designated the Fourth Parallel; and though it was at no time armed as a battery, it was manned at all points with select marksmen.

"Every hour," says Mr. Connolly, "made obvious the necessity for hastening the termination of a struggle which had swallowed up an army in its chequered events. The secret of success in a siege, next to good generalship, is expedition in the construction of essential works, and attention to their efficiency. This was ever borne in mind; and though opposed by astounding obstacles, never a day passed but a sensible addition was made to the vast network of trenches. Parallels and approaches now covered the hills, and saps daringly progressed in front; dingy pits, filled with groups of prying and fatal marksmen, studded the advances and flanks; caves were augmented in size and number in the sides of the ravines, to give safety to the gunpowder; and shell-rooms were constructed to hold the combustibles. All existing batteries were maintained intact, and new works by degrees were thrown up in front to grapple with the sturdy formations of the Russians."

When these works were finished, the masks that blinded those apertures that were to become embrasures were hastily removed, and heavy guns run through them, to flash destruction on the works of the enemy. One hundred and sixty-five guns and mortars of all weights and calibres were got into position, and the average distance of the advanced batteries from the Russian lines was, on the right, for 11 guns and 5 mortars, 360 yards; and on the left, for 20 guns and 3 mortars, about 460 yards.

"It will hardly be credited," says the United Service Magazine, "that while the Sappers were thus exerting and distinguishing themselves - while they formed a sort of perpetual forlorn hope at the head of every parallel, and in every battery, and were constantly eliciting the highest encomiums from Lord Raglan, our jobbing authorities at home wholly excluded them from the distribution of honours!"

"No medals," wrote General Jones, "have been sent out for the Royal Sappers and Miners for distinguished conduct. The strength of the corps serving with the army is equal to any regiment of the line, and therefore the Sappers and Miners should be considered entitled to the same number as has been sent out for a regiment; and by the conduct of so many men who have distinguished themselves, there will not be any difficulty of finding those entitled to them under the royal warrant."

That the dangers of the great siege fell heavily on this scientific corps is attested by their casualties, which, in a body of 935 of all ranks, were no less than 445, or one half of the whole force.

On the 19th of April, a very sharp conflict took place at some of the enemy's rifle-pits, which terminated in our retention of two. The enemy subsequently made an ineffectual attempt to retake them, but were repulsed. This success was not accomplished without the loss of many slain and wounded; among the former were the colonel and an officer of the 77th Regiment, and two of the Royal Engineers. The other three pits retained by the enemy were only twenty yards distant, so the work between them was as close and murderous as musketry well could make it.

The sixth and final bombardment of Sebastopol commenced at dawn on the morning of the 5th of September.

"The air was pure and light, and a gentle breeze from the south-west, which continued all day, drifted over the steppe, and blew gently into Sebastopol. The sun," continues Dr. Russell, "shone serenely, through the vapours of the early morning and wreaths of snowy clouds, on the long lines of white houses inside those rugged defences of earth and gabionade which have so long kept our armies gazing in vain on this august city. The ships floated quietly on the waters of the roads, which were smooth as a mirror; while, outside, our own fleet and that of the French, equally inactive, and not quite so useful to us, were reposing between Kasatch and Constantine, as idly as though they were ' painted ships upon a painted ocean.'"

Notwithstanding the five previous bombardments, Sebastopol still presented, he says, "a stately appearance, as it rises on the hill-side, tier over tier, displaying churches, stately mansions, and public buildings of fine white or red sandstone, with gardens interspersed, and trees growing in the walks. These fine structures are not exempt from 'low neighbourhoods' of whitewashed houses, belonging to the garrison, or to the poorer inhabitants. The hill on which this part of the city stands rises from the rear of the Flagstaff Battery to the height of 200 feet or more; it presents a steep face to the creek from the dockyard, and then sweeps round towards the roadstead, to the level of which it abruptly descends at the rear of the southern forts."

Without waiting for us, the French suddenly commenced to bombard. Close to their Bastion du Mat, there suddenly started into mid-air three pillars of earth and dust, each more than a hundred feet in height, as they exploded three fougasses, or little mines (which are usually placed about eight feet under ground), to blow in the counterscarp, and to serve as a signal for their men to begin.

In an instant, then, from the water of the shining sea to the dockyard creek, there seemed to run a stream of spouting fire three miles in length, as battery after battery shot forth its missiles, and the smoke of "the villainous saltpetre "curled upward in white, fleecy clouds. " The lines of the French trenches

91

were at once covered as though the very clouds of heaven had settled down upon them, and were whirled about in spiral jets, in festoons, in clustering bunches, in columns, and in sheets, all commingled, involved together, and uniting, as it were, in the vehement flames beneath."

From these batteries a ponderous storm of iron burst through the Russian lines, beating down or tearing up everything; gabions were torn to white splinters, and rent asunder; jets of earth and dust started high in air as fascine-baskets were dashed to pieces; and through their lines the round shot went dashing and crashing among the houses in rear of the fast falling defences. Never since cannon were invented had a discharge so simultaneous, so startling, or so tremendous from its actual metal, been given, and hence the Russians seemed for a while utterly paralysed.

Two hundred French guns of large calibre were now being worked with the most frightful energy, enthusiasm, and effect; and the echoes of the cannonade pealing over land and sea, over

French attack on the Malakhoff

hill and through valley, died away only for a moment, to be repeated louder still. Walls of stone, and even of granite, fell down in masses, while those of brick disappeared as if made of stucco; and even the solid earthworks, so long trusted in, began to yawn and show great breaches at last.

With good practice but slow - for their batteries were undermanned - the Russian artillerymen began to return this fire; but harder then worked the French, and with greater rapidity than ever they sent their shot crashing among the churches, terraces, and mansions of Sebastopol.

Meantime, we were not idle; our gallant Naval Brigade and siege-train were also at work, steadily and perseveringly hammering away with shot and shell at the solid face of the Redan, and the high front of the Malakhoff. From Gordon's and Chapman's batteries, the mortars hurled 10- and 13-inch shells over and into the enemy's works, causing a terrible destruction of life -and limb, and connecting the discharge of these by rounds from 32- arid 68-pounder guns.

Our Quarry Battery, armed with two mortars and eight cohorns, distant 400 yards from the Redan, plied the suburb in rear of the Malakhoff Tower vigorously with bombs, and swept the top of the Redan itself with a pitiless storm of round shot and grape, till both these mighty works became alike battered and silent. The faces of all the parapets were pitted with shot and shell, as if they had undergone a species of small-pox; dislodged from their beds, the wooden gabions stuck out fantastically at every imaginable angle; but after two hours and a half of close firing, the French gunners suddenly ceased, to cool their guns, which were becoming dangerously over-heated.

Taking advantage of this lull, the grey-coated Russians were seen creeping out to repair the damage in their works; and from the banquette they threw sandbags over the face of the battered parapet. At ten o'clock, as before, the French exploded some fougasses as a signal, and again the roar of all their guns was heard, with greater fury than ever, and then evident symptoms of agitation were visible in the city, and men with carts and horses were seen hurriedly passing to and fro by the floating bridge that lay between St. Nicholas and St. Michael; and at nine o'clock a great column of infantry crossed over it, to resist any attempt to assault, while a movement towards Inkerman was made by their troops stationed at the Balbek. During nearly the entire day, the shells were whistling through the sky, to explode amid the works or streets of the fated city, and its blue seemed to be scoured by a constant succession of fiery arcs.

Our artillery practice was so perfect that every shell burst just where each gunner wished that it should; and all this time the Russians made but a feeble reply.

At five o'clock, a Russian frigate moored inside the double booms and bridge of boats was seen in flames, and men and officers hailed the event with delight; then as the night darkened, she seemed a grand pyramidal blaze from stem to stern; but

Interior of the Redan after its capture

94

whether she had been fired by the red-hot shot of the French, or - as some thought - by the Russians themselves, as a signal to call in their cavalry from Eupatoria, none in camp could know. "At eight o'clock, the light was so great that the houses of the city, and the forts on the other side, could be distinguished without difficulty. The masts stood long, towering aloft, like great pillars of fire; but one after the other they came down. The decks fell in at ten o'clock, and by midnight the frigate had burned to the water's edge."

On this eventful occasion, our batteries were armed with thirty-four 13-inch mortars, twenty 10-inch ditto, ten 8-inch ditto, and twenty 54 inch cohorns: making a total of ninety-one mortars.

We had sixty-one 32-pounders, thirty-seven 8-inch guns, seven of 10-inch, six 68-pounders, and three nines, for the heads of the saps. We threw in 12,721 bombs and 89,540 round shot.

All the night of the 5th, a steady musketry fire was maintained along the whole front, to prevent the Russians from repairing the damages inflicted during the past day; and at ten p.m., orders were sent to the batteries to open next day as soon as there was sufficient light; but they were limited to fifty rounds per gun. In obedience to this, at half-past five, the whole line of batteries, from the Quarantine to Inkerman, opened fire with a terrific crash; then the agitation in the town soon became more than ever apparent; and the long-range shot from them did considerable mischief. Thus, between the 3rd and 6th, there were killed and wounded in the trenches 246 officers and men.

At sunset on the 6th, the bombardment was renewed, and was continued by the light of the stars, without a moment's intermission, till an hour before dawn. The musketry fire was equally unremitting, as the trench guards had orders to sweep the face of the Russian defences; hence fully 150,000 rounds of ball cartridge were spent upon them every night since the bombardment began.

At daybreak on the 7th, the cannonade was resumed as usual; from the centre of their works the Russians failed to respond; but their Inkerman batteries across the harbour fired briskly on the French, and slew numbers of them. On this morning a high wind blew clouds of grey dust from the town; this mingled with the smoke of its batteries, and caused some difficulty in ascertaining the effect of the fire; but when an opening did occur the amount of ruin and devastation caused by our shot was indeed appalling.

At noon, the generals held a council of war at the British head-quarters, where Pelissier, and General the Marquis de la Marmora, attended. The latter was at the head of the Sardinian contingent, and had early distinguished himself in war - on the heights of Pastrengo, where his happy diversion in rear of the Austrian army enabled that of Piedmont to re-form. To the Allies it became evident that a grand assault was imminent, for after the council broke up, orders were sent to the surgeons to clear out the hospitals, and prepare for the reception of more wounded. The Foot Guards were directed, for that night, to occupy the trenches on the right, to be relieved by the Highlanders in the morning; and that the attack would be made by the Light and 2nd Divisions. "So the night was spent in a fever of expectation and anxiety, amid the roar of the bombardment, which the wind blew in deafening bursts back to the allied camp."

At last came the morning of Saturday, the 8th of September, when, after being for a year before Sebastopol, the columns of the Allies began to form for the grand assault; and many a man who saw that day come in was fated not to see it close.

THE REDAN, 1855

The morning of the assault was a dull, cheerless, and depressing one. From the Euxine a biting wind swept over the land; clouds of white dust, and dusky smoke that came from many a burning ship and blazing street, rose high in the air, above the green, coppered spires and shot-riven batteries of Sebastopol, overhanging the whole city like a sombre pall, through which the sun shone feebly, shorn of all his rays. At last he seemed to fade out, as the vapour thickened, and the whole sky assumed a dull and wintry tint of grey.

All comers from Balaclava and the rear of the camp were stopped by a line of sentinels posted from Inkerman, on the right, to the sea on the left; while a cordon of cavalry vedettes cut off the communication with Cathcart's Hill and the picket-houses in advance of the camp.

Staff-officers, or others with written permission, alone could pass these lines; but though all idlers were kept back from Balaclava, to obtain glimpses of the impending attack, groups of fur-capped Tartars and red-fezzed Turks began to cluster on every knoll that was at a safe distance from cannon-shot. In great masses, 30,000 Frenchmen were forming to assault the Malakhoff, with 5,000 Sardinians to support them; and our 3rd and 4th Divisions began to get under arms in front of their camp.

During this time, the cannonade, which had recommenced at dawn as usual, was of the most tremendous character; and vast gaps were visible in the streets and principal houses, many of which were half-hidden by the sheets of red fire that gushed through every window and aperture; and by the bridge of boats that lay between the north and south side, fugitives were seen to pass by thousands, bearing their sick, their aged, their children, and their valuables; and this melancholy procession continued in sight, defiling there so long as light remained.

The eyes of the British, until the French began to move, were turned to their own point of attack - the Redan; and here we may inform the non-military readers that a Redan, in field fortification, means simply an indented work with lines and faces; but that one at Sebastopol resembled an unfinished square, with two sides meeting at the salient angle in front of the trenches, by which our troops had dug a passage towards it; the remaining space was left open. In the walls of the parapet there were little apartments, admirably constructed, and roofed in with sacks of earth. These, resembling the cabins of a ship in size, appeared to be meant for various purposes - temporary hospitals, the officers on duty, the commandant, &c. One apartment in rear of this great work had a grate and chimney complete. In the sides of the embrasures were excavations to admit of the gunners resting or sleeping beside their guns. When captured, the famous Redan was found, in its area, to present an uneven surface, like the pits of a vineyard filled in. By a series of trenches it communicated with the Malakhoff; and from the commanding position of the latter, it was quite evident that the Redan would be untenable after the tower was taken.

The former communicated, by a road to the right, with an extensive quadrangular building - the Russian barrack, from which it was only distant about a hundred yards. Behind the Redan was one of the coves, called the artillery or dockyard creek, and beyond it was the town.

As the columns of attack formed, the Russians, thick as bees, could be seen clustered about its deeply-cut embrasures, through which cannon of enormous calibre were grimly peering; and their flat caps and bristling bayonets were visible at times along its lines of defence.

At half-past eleven, the Highland Brigade, with all its pipes playing, came in from Kamara, under Brigadier Cameron, and took up its position in reserve at the right attack; and the Guards, also in reserve, were posted on the same side of the Woronzow Road. The 1st Brigade of the 4th Division served as the trench guards of the left attack, and still remained in them.

The 3rd Division was massed on the green hillside, in front of the tents and wigwams which formed its camp, in readiness to support the left attack, if its services were required. It was arranged that the French should attack the Malakhoff at noon, and that as soon as they began, we were to assail the Redan. "All the amateurs and travelling gentlemen, who rather abound here just now," wrote Dr. Russell, "were in a state of great excitement, and dotted the plain, in eccentric attire which revived olden memories of Cowes, and yachting and sea-bathing. They were, moreover, engaged in a series of subtle manoeuvres down in the ravines, to turn the flank of unwary sentries, in order to get to the front; and their success was most creditable to their enterprise and ingenuity."

The cannonade was permitted to languish as the hour of attack drew near; but when the Russians saw our cavalry and troops in front, they began to shell Cathcart's Hill, and their bombs at long ranges greatly disturbed the equanimity of the spectators as, with loud crashes, they sometimes exploded above their heads in mid-air. At last came the moment of attack!

"At five minutes before twelve o'clock," says Dr. Russell, whom it is impossible to resist quoting, "the French, like a swarm of bees, issued from their trenches close to the doomed Malakhoff, scrambled up its face, and were through the embrasures in the twinkling of an eye. They crossed the seven meters of ground which separated them from the enemy at a few bounds; they drifted lightly and quickly as autumn leaves before the wind, battalion after battalion, into the embrasures; and in a minute or two after the head of their column issued from the ditch, the tricolour was floating over the Korniloff bastion. The musketry was very feeble at first - indeed, our Allies took the Russians by surprise; but they soon recovered themselves, and from twelve o'clock till past seven in the evening, the French had to meet and repulse the repeated attempts of the enemy to regain the work, when, weary of the slaughter of his men, who lay in thousands over the exterior of the works, and despairing of success, the Muscovite general withdrew his exhausted legions, and prepared, with admirable skill, to evacuate the place. As soon as the tricolour was observed waving, through the smoke and dust, over the parapet of the Malakhoff, four rockets were sent up from Chapman's battery, as a signal for our assault upon the Redan. They were almost borne back by the violence of the wind, and the silvery jets of sparks they threw out on exploding were scarcely visible against the raw grey sky."

The divisional orders for the 2nd Division were very much the same as those for the Light Division, and the following is the detail of the stormers in the terrible conflict that ensued: -

The covering party consisted of 100 men of the 3rd or Kentish Buffs, led by Captain John Lewes, and 100 of the 2nd Battalion of the Rifles, under Captain Hammond. The scaling-ladder party consisted of 160 of the 3rd Buffs, under Captain F. F. Maude, with 160 of the 77th Regiment, under the gallant Major Welsford.

The part of the force from the 2nd Division consisted of 260 of the Buffs, 300 of the 41st, and 200 of the 62nd, with a working party of 100 men of the 41st. The rest of Windham's brigade, consisting of the 47th and 49th, were in reserve, together with Warren's brigade of the same division, of which the 30th, or Cambridgeshire, and 55th, or Westmoreland, were called into action, and much cut up. Brigadier Shirley was on board ship at this time; but the moment he heard that an assault had been resolved on, he hastened to' his post. In his absence, Colonel Unett, of the 19th, as senior officer, would have had the perilous honour of leading the forlorn hope; and as he was unaware that Shirley meant to come on shore, he had to decide with Colonel Windham as to who should have precedence in the assault. They coolly tossed for it, and Colonel Unett won. He still had it in his power to say whether he would go first, or follow Windham, the Assistant Quarter-Master General.

"My choice is made," said Unett, as he turned over the shilling; "I shall be the first man inside the Redan!"

But fortune ordained it otherwise, as he fell, badly wounded, early in the affair.

"Forward - ladders to the front - eight men per ladder! "were now the orders; and scarcely had the men left the fifth parallel, when the flank guns of the Redan opened upon them as they moved up rapidly to the salient, in which there were no cannon, as the formation of such a work does not permit of their being placed in such a position.

In dark-green uniforms, patched with many a rag, 100 riflemen, bearing the ladders, preceded the stormers, who advanced with a furious run, with bayonets fixed, and rifles at the short trail, while the round shot tore up the earth beneath their feet, or swept men away by entire sections, strewing limbs and fragments of humanity everywhere, when the genuine British "hurrah!" deepening into a species of fierce roar, mingled with the din of the fire-arms and the defiant yells of the Muscovites.

Brigadier Shirley was almost immediately half-blinded by dust, knocked into his eyes by a round shot. This compelled him to retire, and his place was taken by Lieutenant-Colonel Bunbury, of the Welsh Fusiliers, a tried soldier, who had served at the Kohat Pass, and who was next in regimental rank to Unett, who had been already stricken down. Crawling and limping back to the rear or the trenches, for succour and shelter, the wounded groaning and shrieking, were coming in hundreds now, and in less than a minute the whole slope of the Redan was covered with red-coats - the dead or the helpless.

Brigadier Van Straubenzee received a contusion in the face, and was forced to quit the field. The Honourable Colonel Handcock, who led 100 of the Perthshire Regiment, and 200 of the 97th, fell mortally wounded by a ball in the head, and never spoke again. Captain Hammond fell dead, and Major Welsford had his head blown off by a cannon-ball, fired by a Russian officer, who afterwards surrendered himself to a sergeant of the 97th. Captain Grove was severely wounded, and of the commanders of parties, Brigadier Windham, Captains Lewes, Maude, and Fyers alone escaped the volleys of grape and musketry that swept the slope of the Redan.

Colonel Lysons, of the 23rd, though wounded in the thigh, remained on the ground, and with brandished sword, he cheered on the stormers, who had no time to lose, as the Russians from the Malakhoff, inflamed by blood, defeat, and fury, were rushing down in hordes to aid in the defence of the Redan.

In crossing the open space between the head of the trenches and the point of attack, some of the ladders were lost or left behind, in consequence of their bearers being shot down; yet the edge of the ditch was reached, and several planted without much difficulty, till the Russians - at the traverses which enfiladed them at right angles - opened a murderous musketry fire on those who were crossing or scrambling into the embrasures.

The scene in the ditch where the dead and the dying, the bleeding, the panting, and the exhausted, lay over each other three or four deep, was beyond description; and at a place called the Picket-house, was one solitary English lady watching this terrible assault, breathless and pale, putting up prayers with her white lips. Her husband was engaged with the stormers, and soon after his mangled body was borne past her on a stretcher.

The stormers of the Light Division had made straight for the salient and projecting angle of the Redan, at a place where the ditch was fifteen feet deep. The party detailed for the ladders had planted them, but they were found to be too short. Six or seven were there. Led by their officers, the men leaped into the ditch and scrambled up on the other, and scaled the parapet which the Russians deserted to man the breastworks and traverses.

"To show," says Dr. Russell, "what different impressions different people receive of the same matter, let me remark that one officer of rank told me that the Russians visible in the Redan did not exceed 150 men when he got into it. He further expressed an opinion that they had no field-pieces inside the breastworks, from one re-entering angle to the other. A regimental officer, on the other hand, positively assured me that when he got on the top of the parapet of the salient, he saw at about a hundred yards in advance of him, the breastwork with gaps in it, through which were seen the muzzles of field-pieces; and that in rear of it were compact masses of Russian infantry, the front rank kneeling with fixed bayonets, as if prepared to receive cavalry, while the two rear ranks over them kept up a sharp and destructive fire upon our men. The only way to reconcile these discrepancies is to suppose that the first spoke of the earliest stage of the assault, and that the latter referred to a later period, when the Russians may have opened embrasures in the breastwork, having been reinforced by the fugitives from the Malakhoff, and by troops behind the barracks in its rear."

Most unfortunately now, our men, when they reached the crest of the parapet, instead of following their officers, and rushing on the enemy, as stormers ought to do, with the charged bayonet and clubbed musket, commenced independent file-firing. The small party of the 90th and 97th, much diminished now, certainly went gallantly on towards the breastwork; but they were too weak to force it; they had to retire and get behind the traverses, at which the men of several regiments were now congregated, and keeping up a brisk fire on the Russians, whose flat caps or round glazed helmets were visible above the breastwork. By a rapidly increasing flank and direct fire, converging on the salient, the Russians had greatly diminished our force; and as we were weakened, they were strengthened by parties from both re-entering angles. The 3rd Buffs and 41st Welsh poured in through the embrasures, immediately after the men of the 90th and 97th, till the overwhelming masses of the enemy made a rush on our men with the bayonet, and drove them into an angle of the work, and ultimately over the parapet to the exterior slope, where the fragments of many corps of the Light and 2nd Divisions were all wedged together, firing into the Redan as long as their ammunition lasted, and as long as cartridges from the rear could be handed to those in front.

An hour and a half of this disastrous conflict had passed, the Russians having cleared the Redan of all but our dead, but not yet being in possession of its parapets, when they made a second charge with their bayonets under a heavy musketry fire; and throwing great quantities of large stones, grape, and small round shot, from the hand, drove those in front back upon the men in the rear, who were tumbled headlong into the ditch. The wooden gabions in the parapet now gave way, and rolled down with those who were upon them; and the men in rear, thinking that all was lost, retired into the fifth parallel, but many were buried alive in the ditch by falling earth, and perished miserably.

To the trenches there was a fearful run for life, the men "rolling over like rabbits" and lying over each other four deep, to escape the leaden tempest that was raining on them; but speedily recovering breath, they opened a heavy and continuous fire on the parapets of the Redan. Captain Preston, and Lieutenants Swift and Wilmer of the 90th, were lying dead inside the fatal place, with a hecatomb of others. Individual deeds of daring were too frequent to be particularised. "The men of the 41st who rushed into the Redan with Colonel Windham, were named Hartnady, Kennelly, and Dan Mahoney; the last, a fine tall grenadier, fell dead in the embrasure by Colonel Windham's side, shot through the heart, as he was shouting, 'Come on, boys, come on!' His blood spouted over those near him."

General Codrington, though the salient was held by our men for one hour and fifty-six minutes, would seem to have become confused by the failure of the attack, and to have lost, for the time, I the coolness that usually characterised him. He was hesitating about sending more men to the front, or he was unable to form a nucleus of resistance and attack; hence we lost the Redan, and our men, pressed by numbers, by the bayonet, and by showers of musketry, together with the fire of field-pieces, were hurled, as stated, over the parapet and back upon their own trenches. Colonel James Eman of the 41st, "one of the best officers in the army - a man of singular calmness and bravery, who was beloved by his officers and men, and whose loss was lamented by all who knew him," was shot through the lungs while in the act of rallying the Welsh Regiment. His sword-arm was uplifted at the moment the ball struck him, and when he was carried to the rear, a surgeon assured him that his lungs were uninjured.

"I know better," said he with a sad smile, "and know that such hopes are vain - I am bleeding internally."

He died that night. Two captains of the 41st fell with him, Corry and Lockhart.

Captain Hume, of the 55th, was blown up by a shell, and yet was not severely wounded.

The attack was to be resumed at five in the morning by the Guards and Highlanders, under Sir Colin Campbell, the future Lord Clyde; but the Redan was evacuated in the night. The person who made this discovery was Corporal John Ross, of the Royal Sappers and Miners. He was searching outside for wounded comrades, when falling in with two under the abatis, he observed the absence of the Russian outpost; and leaving his canteen with the wounded, he crept cautiously forward, climbed the slope and entered the Redan. The last standing-ground of the enemy was unguarded and vacant, and, returning joyfully to the trenches, he reported the great news that the Russians had flown.

By this time, fort after fort in Sebastopol had been blown into the air, each with a shock as if the earth were being torn in twain. The sky seemed full of live shells, which burst in thousands like scarlet rockets. Columns of dark smoke seemed to prop heaven like dusky pillars as they rose above the city, whose defenders in thousands, without beat of drum, or blast of bugle, poured away in a vast multitude by the bridge of boats. When the last Russian soldier had passed, the chains of the mighty pontoon, a quarter of a mile in length, were slashed through, and it swung

A street in Sebastopol after the siege

heavily over to the other side when we were in full possession of Sebastopol.

They left the town with its barracks, palaces, theatres, arsenals, stores, and port, sheeted with lire; the flames lit up all the roadsteads, where, one after another, the scuttled Russian ships were seen disappearing in quick succession beneath the flame-tinted waters of the inner harbour.

Many of our officers were found in the Redan with a hand clutching a Russian's throat, or coat, or belt; man grasping man in a fierce and last embrace. Captain Hammond, of the Rifles, was found next morning in the ditch, beneath a heap of slain, with a bayonet-wound in his heart; he had only arrived from England three days before. Some of our dead soldiers were actually found clinging to the parapet and slope of the glacis, as if still alive: thus attesting the reluctance with which they retired, and the desperation with which they died before that fatal place, which we should never have attacked at all, but should have aided the French in the capture of the Malakhoff, after which event it must have fallen, as being no longer tenable.

There was a great feeling of depression in the camp all night. It was quite uncertain what the result might be before the Redan was discovered to be empty. All that the troops knew was, that the French were in the Malakhoff, and that our attempt had failed. "It was an eventful night; the camp was full of wounded men, the hospitals were crowded, and sad stories ran from mouth to mouth respecting the losses of the officers and the behaviour of the men."

An immense number of the Russian dead in front were found to be officers.

Many of our men were now mere recruits, and in some instances were scarcely a match for the well-trained veterans of Russia. Some who were serving in the ranks of the 4th Division, "had only been enlisted a few days," says Dr. Russell," and had never fired a rifle in their lives!" and a siege where a man learns chiefly to ensconce himself behind gabions and sand-bags, and steal quiet "pot-shots," without exposing himself unnecessarily, is perhaps the worst kind of military service to develop courage, confidence, and hardihood in a young soldier.

One of the most heroic episodes here was connected with a mere youth, named Massy, a lieutenant of the 19th Regiment, who kept out in the open in the hope of inducing the soldiers to follow, and there, amidst the most dreadful fire, he stood with a reckless courage that excited the astonishment even of the enemy; he was terribly wounded, but won the sobriquet of "Redan Massy." Leaving the service, he resumed his studies at the. University of Dublin, where the students presented him with a magnificent sword.

"The secret of the attack was admirably preserved," says Major Rankin - the last officer killed in the Crimea - in his journal. "Not a whisper was circulated. It took us all by

Sweaborg

surprise, as we imagined no further attempt would be made on the Redan, after the failure of the assault of June 18th. We heard, however, that it was arranged that both armies should 'go in' in earnest, and that the success of the French in their attack on the Malakhoff was to be the signal for our advance I on our old enemy, the Redan. I prepared myself, as well as the short interval permitted, for the probable fate that would attend the performance of the desperate duty. I took farewell of my mother and all my relations, committing them to the protection and the blessing of God. I earnestly endeavoured to pray, and to compose my mind. I felt the only course open was willing submission, and fixed resolve that, if I were to die, to fall in endeavouring to do my duty to the uttermost. Beyond this I was determined not to go, though every soldier should expose himself without the slightest hesitation to the greatest danger when necessary, recklessness should never form any part of his creed. No really good soldier throws his life away without aim or object"

- C H A P T E R   I X -

BOMBARDMENT OF SWEABORG, 1855

Exactly a month before the attack on the Redan, Admiral Dundas, who had succeeded Sir Charles Napier in command of the Baltic fleet, inflicted a severe blow upon Russia by the bombardment of Sweaborg.

The latter is an important imperial fortress in the Gulf of Finland, three miles south-east of Helsingfors, from the quays of which, says Dr. Milner, its ramparts of massive granite may be seen, with the roofs of the buildings it contains; these consist of barracks, magazines, prisons, and a limited number of private houses; it completely commands the seaward passage to the city, or the narrow Gustav-Sound, the only channel which has water deep enough for large vessels. The fortifications extend over six different islands. Five of these are connected by bridges, and occupy a space of about 1,200 yards by 650. The isle of Vargon is somewhat central and is considered the citadel. The only practicable passage between lies by Treksholm and Gustafsvard. All these islands bristle with cannon and are grim with strong ramparts. The works, which are of granite, and are as massive as the foundations on which they are built, being for the most part constructed out of the solid rock, are supposed to be armed with 810 pieces of cannon, and have casemates for about 7,000 muskets, and barracks for a garrison of 12,000 men.

Such are the defences for Helsingfors, the new capital of Finland, and these make Sweaborg the Gibraltar of the North. Sir Charles Napier pronounced the place to be, like Cronstadt, impregnable by sea as well as by shore. To land troops so long as there were batteries unsilenced, and casemates full of riflemen, would have been most disastrous, as all the batteries flank each other, and the channels between were closed by sunken ships, granite blocks, and dismounted cannon.

On the 6th of August, Admiral Dundas, accompanied by Admiral Seymour, left Norgen, and the same day came to anchor off Sweaborg, when the French fleet, under Admiral Penaud, formed a junction with ours. The attack was contemplated for the 7th, but Admiral Penaud suggested that if a mortar battery was constructed on the island of Langorn, it would greatly facilitate the success of the operations, which were delayed until that work was affected.

Admiral Penaud thereupon raised a sand-bag battery, on which he mounted four of the best British 13-inch mortars. It was completed on the 9th. On the previous day, the imperial standard was seen to float over both Sweaborg and Helsingfors, which caused a rumour that either the emperor or one of the grand dukes had come. On the 9th it disappeared; but crowds of persons from Helsingfors and the shores of Finland were upon the batteries, gazing eagerly upon the mighty fleet which covered the waters before them - the same powerful armament which we have so lately described at the bombardment of Bomarsund.

On the morning of the 9th, at a quarter to seven o'clock, a signal from the flagship ordered, "Gun and mortar vessels, open fire with shell."

Three-quarters of an hour elapsed before the first bomb went hissing on its fiery errand. The whole line promptly followed, and a blaze of fire girdled the granite wall of Sweaborg. The distance assumed was 3,600 yards; but the gun-boats ran in 500 yards nearer, shot their missiles and retired steaming round in a circle, somewhat in the way practised by the ships at the bombardment of Rangoon and Odessa. Their perpetual motion thus rendered it impossible for the Russian gunners to keep a precise range, while a galling fire was poured upon their works,

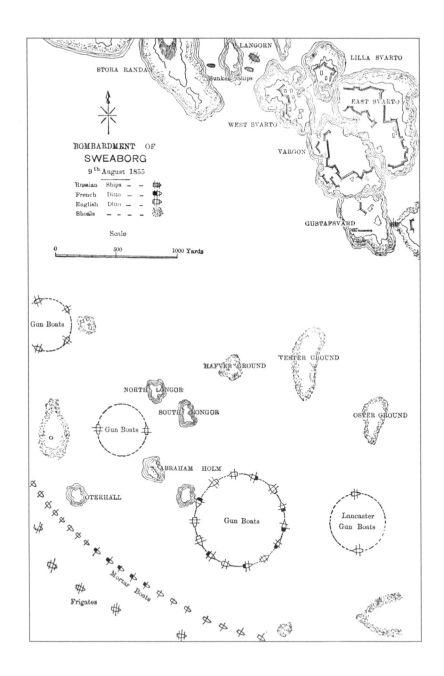

BOMBARDMENT OF
SWEABORG
9th August 1855

Russian   Ships
French   Ditto
English   Ditto
Shoals

Scale

0   500   1000 Yards

STORA RANDA

LANGORN

Sunken Ships

LILLA SVARTO

EAST SVARTO

WEST SVARTO

VARGON

GUSTAFSVARD

Gun Boats

HAFVER GROUND

VESTER GROUND

NORTH LONGOR

SOUTH LONGOR

OSTER GROUND

Gun Boats

ABRAHAM HOLM

OTERHALL

Gun Boats

Lancaster
Gun Boats

Mortar Boats

Frigates

112

almost with impunity. Before describing the action in detail, some remarks upon the cannonade are necessary.

"What our navy accomplished at Sweaborg," says Nolan, "was very important; they made havoc by vertical firing among the troops, and thus caused a heavy loss to the Russian army; they both by a vertical and sweeping fire injured the cannon, broke the port-holes, and otherwise damaged the batteries; they demolished the splendid barracks, and all the destructible material of war contained upon the islands; and by the explosion of a magazine, whole batteries and their guns were blown into the air, and all this was accomplished without any loss of life or ship ; about four officers and no men wounded, was the computation of casualties. Our readers must not suppose, however, that Sweaborg might, in the result of such a bombardment, have fallen into the hands of the Allies, or that the power of the garrison was so broken, that the fleet could approach its granite rocks with impunity. Had Admiral Dundas sent his line-of-battle ships within range of the fortifications, he could not have brought them in safety away; some must have been sunk or blown up. Our readers must not, therefore, be surprised to hear that the Russians offered a Te Deum for the victory at Sweaborg. They treated it as a repulse of the Allies, although the repulse of an attack from which the garrison suffered heavily."

Finding that the circular action of the gun and mortar boats baulked their aim, the Russian gunners became somewhat disquieted. They lost confidence, and their fire, which was delivered at first with energy, began to slacken.

After three hours' bombarding, a mountain of fire suddenly gushed up in the centre of the principal island, when the large magazine exploded. Had the isle been torn from its granite base in the sea, the roar of that explosion could not have been more terrific or astounding. Far over the echoing land and sea went the report, and the crowds upon the neighbouring shores supposed that by some mighty element new in war, the whole of the isles and batteries had been destroyed at once.

This explosion, which sent massive walls, heavy cannon, and shattered corpses into the air together, combined with the disheartening conviction that they could not obtain the range of those pestilent gunboats, some of whose names were very peculiar - the Badger, Pelter, Snap, Weasel, Pincher, Biter, Snapper, &c. - so disheartened the Russian gunners that their fire slackened for some hours.

Yet suddenly, as if inspired by some new hope, or animated by some fresh expedient, they renewed their efforts with great energy; but they had not long recommenced their fierce cannonade, when another of their magazines exploded, and again the sound of thunder rattled long and continuously over land and sea to vast distances. This was about noon.

Iron balls, live shells, thousands of muskets, house-roofs, and every description of material, ascended in a dark storm into mid-air, to crash downward in a shower among the garrison, killing and wounding men on every hand; and by setting fire to every combustible material, causing hundreds of minor explosions; hence, by the time that everything inflammable was ignited, the isles resembled a veritable Pandemonium.

The crews of the line-of-battle ships who were crowded in the tops, the cross-trees, and out upon the yards, cheered these results with the utmost ardour and excitement; and the view obtained of the blazing barracks, magazines, and other edifices, was indeed sublime. The lesser war-steamers made efforts to come near the sphere of action.

The Amphion, Hastings, and Comwallis, at one and the same instant, threw in their broadsides; while the Cossack, Cruiser, and Arrogant poured their fire upon one of the isles where the troops of the garrison seemed to be chiefly collected.

To the sublimity of the occasion was now added the mighty thunder of the cannonade from these larger ships; but their range was too remote to prove very effectual. The firing was continued until eight in the evening, without the least cessation on the part of the assailants; while the Russian guns were worked unequally - fiercely at times, as if the defenders were inspired by sudden hope or energy, and anon languidly, when confusion - even terror - seemed to pervade the garrison. There were many merchantmen, steam and sailing ships, which had been armed for the defence, several gun-boats, and some men-of-war; but all these shared the fiery destruction which overwhelmed the magazines, houses, and barracks; so the marine forces shared in the disorder and discomfiture of the troops on the isles.

After eight p.m., our mortar-vessels withdrew, many of their mortars having been disabled by incessant firing, and being no longer serviceable. At that time the islands resembled the craters of volcanoes, gushing red fires upwards into the darkening sky - powder and bombs from time to time hurling upward whatever came within the reach of their explosive force. During the whole night, we are told, "the scene was, therefore, one of awful grandeur, striking every one who saw, or performed a part in the terrible drama, with the dreaded sublimity of war."

The night of the 9th was comparatively quiet on the part of the attacking force, their mortars having become literally too hot for use.

On the following day, the bombardment was resumed with similar results; and during the night the rocket-boats filled all the sky between themselves and the shore with arches of fire, till day dawned again on land and sea. The fleet had not a sufficient number of these boats, or bomb-ketches, or, as Sir Charles Napier afterwards asserted in London, not one stone in Sweaborg would have been left upon another. "To the shame of the British Admiralty, the admiral was left without the means of completing his work."

During two days and nights, and part of a third day, the British guns hurled 1,000 tons of iron balls and shells into an area of three square miles, consuming in doing so, 100 tons of gunpowder; while the loss of the Allies was the most trivial ever sustained in inflicting a chastisement so terrible on an enemy; only one British sailor was killed and one wounded!

In Sweaborg, the whole of the government buildings, barracks, magazines, and stores were destroyed; twenty-three ships set on fire by shells; and rockets sheeted the sky with flames, though the Russians assert that only one man - a Cossack of course - was killed, more than a thousand of them were put hors de combat.

After the bombardment terminated, great alarm was felt for Helsingfors as well, after the dreadful damage caused By the Allied guns at Sweaborg; but Admiral Dundas was loth to attack the place, for the sake of the innocent people and their beautiful cathedral, which would inevitably have perished.

In the bombardment of Sweaborg the duty was most arduous, and the conduct of officers and men meritorious - none more so, perhaps, than those of the Royal Marine Artillery; and after the dreadful and incessant booming of the guns for such a length of time, most of the men in the fleet remained deaf for many hours - even for two days - after it had ceased.

- C H A P T E R   X -

KINBURN, 1855

In October it was resolved to reduce the Russian fort at Kinburn, where it occupies a narrow tongue of land at the mouth of the Dnieper, opposite to Otshakov.

Its peninsular situation renders it a place of great strength; but with the disadvantage of having no fresh water. Below this fortress - the scene of one of Suvaroff's memorable victories in 1787 - are several houses occupied by Russian peasants and fishermen.

The Black Sea fleet weighed and stood along the shore, to the great alarm of the inhabitants, whose snug villages, immense herds grazing on the green slopes, and their well-filled farmyards were distinctly visible as it came to anchor about three miles westward of the fort.

This was on the 14th of October.

The troops for the expedition consisted of a body of Sappers and Miners, the Land Transport Corps, artillery and cavalry.

The 17th, 20th, 21st, and 57th Regiments formed the 1st Brigade; the 2nd was composed of the 63rd Regiment, and two battalions of Royal Marines. They were all landed from the line-of-battle ships in the launches and paddle-box boats, towed by the small steamers with light draught of water. The following were the orders issued : -

"No. 1. The line-of-battle ships to engage the Fort of Kinburn and two sand-bag batteries on the point, will anchor in about thirty feet, in a line extending northward from the fort, bearing east, and about 1,200 yards from it.

"No. 2. The four French line-of-battle ships to form the southern division, so that the Montebello will be the fourth ship from the south, and the Royal Albert, as the fifth ship, will be the southern ship of the British division."

The nine ships were ordered to be in a position for the first five or six to engage Kinburn, at about 1,200 yards or less; the rest to take the sand-bag batteries in flank and rear at about 1,000 yards. The three French floating-batteries to be in a line about 600 yards from the fort.

The mortar-vessels to anchor at 2,800 yards' distance, with the fort bearing north-east. The Sidon, Curacoa, Tribune, Dauntless, and Terrible, were to anchor off the north sand-bag battery; the paddle-steamers to anchor between the line-of-battle ships, for the purpose of firing steadily on the embrasures of the casemates. The gun-boats covered the landing of the troops, and the Admiral held captains responsible "for there being no firing unless the men can see distinctly the objects they are directed to fire upon."

On the night of the 14th, the Valorous, Captain Buckle, with Rear-Admiral Sir Houston Stewart on board, and several British and French vessels, forced the passage between Otshakov and the peninsula of Kinburn, and got into Dnieper Bay.

Without the least opposition from the governor, old Major-General Kokonovitch, our 17th was the first regiment ashore. The mortar and gun-boats then bombarded the works heavily for three hours, without producing any serious impression. The weather was fine and clear, so the troops set to work cheerily, entrenching themselves on the sandy peninsula, while some Cossack lancers were seen hovering in the distance about Cherson.

On the morning of the 16th, a few French dragoons, when patrolling in front of the lines towards Cherson, came upon a Cossack picket, lurking" among the lofty brushwood. They gallantly charged at once and put the picket to flight, cutting down , two and capturing two others.

The breeze and surf caused great difficulty in getting stores landed, and some of the paddle-box boats and flats, which drifted on shore, soon settled down in the sand, and one fell under the fire of the fort. At three in the afternoon of this day the steamers and gun-boats opened upon Kinburn again, at the rate of two heavy guns per minute. The Russians replied by their shells, most of which burst high in the air.

"The works are beginning to assume shape and to gather strength with every shovel-throw of earth," wrote Dr. Russell, "so that in a couple of days the Russians will find entrenchments between them and Kinburn whichever way they turn. The entrenched camp will present one line of works towards the fort, and another about half a mile in the rear towards Cherson, the flanks being open to the sea at each extremity, so as to be covered by the guns of the shipping. The French take the trench facing Kinburn, and may be considered as the army of operation against the place - the British guard the rear against any attack from Cherson. It would seem as if the French were going to proceed against the obstinate old Governor of Kinburn

Bombardment of Sweaborg

119

by regular approaches, and to sap up within battering distance, if he holds out in spite of the fleet."

Kokonovitch made a desperate defence.

Early on the morning of the 17th, perceiving that the French had, during the night, crept closer to his batteries and were busy digging their first parallel within 700 yards, he opened a heavy fire on them from some guns that were en barbette on the eastern curtain, and the French responded with their field-pieces.

The morning was dull and grey; the wind was off the shore, and the sea was still and waveless. The floating-batteries, gun and mortar boats, were getting up their steam, and by nine o'clock they opened on the south side of the fort. The three floating-batteries took up a position against the casemates, while the gun-boats fought those batteries whose cannon were en barbette, that is, exposed on the slope of the bastion, and not run through embrasures.

The crash of our shot was terrible; but the Russians were not slow in replying and the whole sea was lashed into foam by the snow-white pillars or spouts made by the falling cannon-shot. About eleven o'clock a fire broke out in the Russian barracks within the fort, and spread from one end of it to the other, the conflagration by its heat and smoke driving the enemy from their guns. Explosions of ammunition were now heard from time to time, and at a quarter past eleven the Russian ensign - St. Andrew's cross - was shot away and not re-hoisted.

At that crisis, the firing from the enormous guns with which the fleet was armed, was tremendous.

Sir Houston Stewart, in the Valorous, and the French admiral, in the Asmodie, came round the Spit Battery into Cherson Bay, followed by eleven steamers, delivering broadsides and engaging the batteries as they passed. They were preceded by the Hannibal, "which ripped up Kinburn with her broadsides." Fed by constant bombs and rockets, more terrible did the fire become, and at half-past twelve another conflagration broke out in the devoted fort.

At the same instant, the towering Valorous, the Asmodie, and the heavy steam-frigates, approaching in stately magnificence, took up their positions off the seaward face of the fort, which was now sorely battered and defaced by the floating-batteries and gun-vessels. The storm of this great ordnance was awfully grand; the very earth seemed to be beaten into dust, and the embers of the blazing barracks rose in fiery columns skyward above the curtains and bastions.

Bravely did the Russians handle the only guns that remained to them; heavier grew the broadsides, and death and carnage, wounds and suffering, were increasing fast in Kinburn.

At last, a single man waved a white flag from the ramparts; then the firing ceased, and boats, with white flags of truce in their sterns, shot off shoreward, to return with tidings that the garrison would capitulate. Admiral Sir Houston Stewart landed near the battery, where he found the French general advancing to parley with General Kokonovitch, who came forth with a sword and pistol in his right hand, and a pistol in his left.

He cast his sword on the ground, and discharged the pistol into the earth, in token of surrender. He was full of rage and bitterness, and shed tears.

"Oh, Kinburn! Kinburn! "he exclaimed, as he left the fort; "Glory of Suvaroff and my shame, I abandon you!"

The garrison, consisting of the 29th Regiment and some artillerymen - in all 1,100 men - marched into the lines. Many of them were tipsy, and when ordered to pile arms, they dashed their muskets with execrations at the feet of their conquerors. The second in command, Saranovitch, a Pole, inflamed by vodka and fury, declared that "he would not surrender, and that he was prepared to blow up the magazine before the enemy should enter."

121

The march past

To have done so after they had entered might have made his vengeance more complete. In this madness he was abetted by two officers, one of the Engineers and another of the Artillery. Amid the thunder of the fleet, the fierce hiss of the flaming rockets, the crash of falling buildings, the smoke and flames of others that were on fire, the Russians had held a hurried council of war, prior to their surrender, and the majority decided that they should do so - the fanatical Saranovitch, the artilleryman, and engineer alone dissenting.

"We can hold out for a week," said they.

"What then?" asked old Kokonovitch; "you have not been able to fire a shot for three-quarters of an hour. Are you likely to be in a better state two hours hence? And above all, where, and how, are our men to live in the meantime?"

So the white flag of truce was displayed - terms given and accepted to the satisfaction of all; but Kokonovitch, who was a brave and high-spirited veteran, wept and covered his furrowed face with his hands, as he flung away the pen with which he signed the terms of surrender.

By these, "the garrison were permitted to retire with everything except their arms, ammunition, and cannon; the officers were allowed to wear their swords, the men to carry off their knapsacks, clothing, regimental bugles, church property, relics, and pictures."

When Kokonovitch was asked to use his influence that no harm might befall such of the allied troops as might enter Kinburn, he replied -

"I shall do so with pleasure; but, at the same time, I must inform you that the flames of the burning barracks are, at this moment, very near the grand magazine."

Saranovitch and the two fanatics who adhered to him, finding themselves in a disgraceful minority, abandoned their suicidal resolutions, and so Kinburn became ours, as far as the flames and smoke would allow us to occupy it. The defenders of the northern forts on the peninsula were not aware for some time of the reduction of the chief works, or disregarded the fact, and continued to blaze away from one large gun, till a shot from the Terrible tumbled the whole casemate about their ears.

In Kinburn Fort were sixty-one pieces of cannon and twelve mortars; of these we dismounted twenty-nine by smashing, or otherwise disabling either the piece or its carriage. They were all long eighteen- or twenty-four-pounders, of great thickness and ancient date. In the central and northern batteries were twenty pieces of cannon, five of which we disabled.

The prisoners were sent to Constantinople in the course of the day. Before departing they sold their kits, and all they could bring to the hammer, officers' droskies, horses, spare clothing, and everything else, by public auction on the beach.

"The officers," says the Times correspondent, "bore their misfortunes with dignity, as was evident from their grave demeanour and stern countenances. Few of them wore decorations, and only one was dressed in full uniform. A chef de bataillon, wearing a long light blue cloak with a red collar, who limped along with difficulty, had a good deal of influence over those around him, and kept the drunken soldiers in awe by his look; and a sergeant, in a long green frock coat with yellow facings and stripes, aided him in repressing the mirthful disposition of some of the bacchanalians on the line of march."

Many of the Russians who embarked were completely intoxicated.

Meanwhile, in the camp before Sebastopol, most conflicting and distressing rumours prevailed concerning our victorious expedition to Kinburn; among these, the smallest were, that the 21st Scots Fusiliers and 57th Regiment had been totally cut to pieces.

CLOSE OF THE CAMPAIGN;
"OUR GRAVES IN THE CRIMEA"

Sebastopol with its magnificent docks being completely destroyed, Russia, on finding herself now fully crippled in the Baltic as well as in the Black Sea, was fain to sue for peace with the Allied Powers ; thus, on the 28th of February, 1856, there were brought to our camp the gladsome tidings that an armistice had been concluded. By telegraph from St. Petersburg, the Russian troops heard of it first; and at eight o'clock, a.m., on that day, a boat bearing a flag of truce put off from the north side of the harbour, and half-way across was met by a French one.

The Russians brought a communication of the armistice from General Luders, and the mail from Constantinople, at a little later period, gave its confirmation to the Allies; and it was arranged that at ten on the following day, there should be a meeting of the Russian and Allied officers at the Tratkir Bridge, to arrange distinctly the terms of the truce that was to succeed a war so vengeful and so bitter. The final treaty of peace was signed at Paris in March, and on Wednesday, the 2nd of April, by a salute of one hundred and one pieces of cannon, the announcement was pealed from the heights of Sebastopol, over the plain of Balaclava, and across the waters of the Euxine, by the artillery of our Light Division; from the Sardinian redoubts at Fedukhine; from the French guns at the Quartier General; and by all the men-of-war at Kazatch and Romiesch.

No salvo of joy rang from the cannon of the humbled Russians, who heard those thunder-peals in stern and moody silence, showing but little satisfaction in the peace their government had been, at last, compelled to seek. The Tchernaya was, for the time, assigned as the limit beyond which the soldiers of the allied army were not to straggle.

The 11th of April saw preparations making for the evacuation of the fatal Crimea, when all were longing for home, and the rest that home alone can give. The expended cannon-shot were being fast collected by the troops, and about 4,000 daily were brought in by the men of each division. Rumour stated that our Guards would probably be the first British troops to quit the land of their suffering, endurance, and glory.

"Alas! how many will lie here till the judgment day?" wrote one of our warriors; "who can tell how many have perished whose lives might have been spared; how many an unknown grave has been untenanted; how many a life wasted which ought to have been saved to the country, to friends, and to an honoured old age! These questions may never be answered, least of all are they likely to be answered at Chelsea Hospital, where the very banners would fall with leaden weight upon the heads of those who would speak the truth that is in them. Heaven lets loose all its plagues on those who delight in war, and on those who shed men's blood, even in the holiest of causes."

And such must have been the emotion of many a British soldier, in many an age, when at the close of a long and desperate struggle, quitting the land of his own glory and of many a comrade's grave on the continent of Europe, in Asia, America, Africa, and the torrid Indian isles; wherever is now heard the sound of "the Queen's morning drum'" - the drum that is beaten round all the world. The Indian mutiny was not then foreseen, and the Russian strife being over, the chief topic in the camp, now about to be broken up forever, was the future destination of the various regiments.

In the middle of April there took place a grand review of the British and French armies, before the Russian. General Luders;

and a most imposing sight it was, as the war-worn, embrowned, and now thoroughly veteran battalions denied past him in their faded uniforms, with the tatters of their shot-riven colours flying over them. The General came attended by a staff of nearly eighty Russian officers, and all spoke of the appearance of our army in terms of the greatest admiration. "Marshal Pelissier was particularly struck with the appearance of the Highland Brigade, which formed a living wall from, the head-quarters camp to the commencement of. the formation of our line, and he declared 'that they were the finest-looking soldiers in the world.'"

The review of the French had taken place earlier in the day. They were formed in loose order, yet their formation was massive, as they passed in battalions at close order, and presented a fine appearance.

Towards the end of May, our whole army was on the move. The 3rd Division was completely broken up, and the Mediterranean stations, some of which had been garrisoned by militia regiments from Britain, began once more to fill with the returning troops. The departure of General Delia Marmora and his picturesque Sardinians was marked by many demonstrations of the regard and esteem in which our army held them. On the day they embarked, all our shipping hoisted the Sardinian flag; the yards of the Leander were manned, and the moment the General set his foot on her deck, there rang from sea to shore three hearty English hurrahs. With the Sardinians we had no past wars to inspire emotions of rivalry. "Their position at Fedukhine," we are told, "brought them into constant contact with the French and Highlanders, and they have left behind them many kindly remembrances not readily to be forgotten."

The fighting over, duty relaxed, and the day of departure, too probably forever, drawing near, our soldiers laboured for weeks to leave behind them affectionate memorials to the memory of those who had fallen.

They could handle their weapons better than the sculptor's chisel and mallet, these gallant fellows, yet ere long the whole Chersonese was covered with stones marking isolated graves, with larger burial-grounds and detached cemeteries from Balaclava to the edge of Sebastopol harbour. "Ravine and plain, hill and hollow," says Russell, "the roadside and the secluded valley from the sea to the Tchernaya, present those stark white stones, singly or in groups, stuck upright in the arid soil or just peering over the rank vegetation which springs from beneath them."

The burial-ground of the non-commissioned officers of our Brigade of Guards was enclosed by a strong wall, built by the hands of their comrades. It was entered by a handsome double gate, ingeniously formed of wood and iron hoops, hammered out straight. These were hinged to pillars of massive hewn stone, each surmounted by a cannon-ball. Within are six rows of graves, each row containing thirty or more bodies. Before the gate was placed a stone cross on four massive blocks, on one of which was carved, - "Grenadiers, Coldstreams, Scots Fusilier Guards, a.d. 1856." The most solitary of all these many memorials, is one - a white sandstone cross - in the plain below which the Turks encamped. It is raised to the memory of Colonel Balfour Ogilvie, "erected by his brother officers."

Sepulchral memorials of our Peninsular and other armies, there are few or none: but the hastily made graveyards of the Crimea, show that the departing Allies. Left a ghastly garrison to keep forever possession of the ground their valour had won.

The day eventually came when the last of our troops were to leave; and here again it is impossible to resist quoting Russell.

"As the Calcutta cleared out of the harbour, the crews of the Leander and Sanspareil gave the gallant ship and her cargo three cheers spontaneously - an unusual compliment from men-of wars' men. The Hussars returned the cheers, and in a few moments more the shores of the Crimea were fading from the view with the last rays of the setting sun lighting the frowning cliffs of Cape Aya, and burnishing up the copper-coloured rocks which line the rugged coast. The men relapsed into silence.

"'How happy should I be, only I'm thinking of the poor fellows we leave behind,' said a soldier, after a pause.

"Yes! but they did their work, and we have no cause to be ashamed of them, thank God!' was the reply of his comrade, 'and so good-bye to the Crimea!'"

The Tartar shepherds of that peninsula, ignorant, barbarous, and avaricious, have in one or two instances violated a handsome tomb in the hope of finding plunder; but with these exceptions, the graves of our fallen soldiers have been faithfully respected by the fierce, yet gallant Russians, who held them so long at bay; and, after the lapse of nearly twenty years, when he visited the spot General Adye was able to report, with Colonel Gordon, that "As regards the alleged desecration of the tombs, we found that the natural destruction, caused by time and weather, has been far greater than any by the hand of man."

Irrespective of far scattered graves upon the dreary plateau, and in the now silent valleys, so long occupied by our troops, may be counted 130 cemeteries, where the bones of our British soldiers lie; and it has been thought more consonant to our national taste to let them sleep in peace where their comrades laid them, than to imitate the French, who have collected more than 28,000 of their dead into one great Campo Santo.

"The large monument upon Cathcart's Hill - which lifts its head high into the air, and may be seen for miles at sea - will long survive the lesser grave-stones which surround it," says a recent writer; "but when every fabric raised by man shall have disappeared, the mounds of turfed earth will proclaim, like the tumulus still visible on the plain of Marathon, that below rest the ashes of men who died nobly for their country."

- C H A P T E R X I I -

BOMBARDMENT OF MOHAMMERAH, 1856

The close of the Crimean war saw some changes introduced in the British service. In every instance the old smooth-bore musket was superseded by the rifle, the weight of which, as fixed by the Hythe Musketry School on the 1st of January 1860, with bayonet fixed, was 10lb. 3.75oz.; and the weight of sixty rounds of ball-cartridge, with seventy-five percussion caps, was 5lb. 8oz. 4drs. As all our infantry with the new weapon were drilled as riflemen, the grenadier and light companies of regiments were assimilated with those of the battalion. The old swallow-tailed coat - the last relic of the coat of the Revolution, and Anne's wars - gave place to the tunic; and all epaulettes and wings were, in some instances, most unwisely abolished; their retention in corps having large head-dresses, such as Guards and Highlanders, being necessary as a matter of taste and costume.

In 1856, all regiments serving in India and the tropics were ordered to adopt light summer frocks in lieu of shell-jackets, with facings and shoulder-straps bearing the regimental number.

Among the operations consequent on a petty war with Persia in this year, when our forces marched against that old ally of Russia, taking Herat and Bushire, and our fleet sailed up the Persian Gulf, was the bombardment of Mohammerah, with the capture of the camp and forts there.

The Persians are not a maritime people. Certain practices of the religion, which cannot be performed at sea, preclude them from venturing on ocean expeditions. The seaboard of the country is small, yet it offers great advantages to traders. The Persian Gulf and the Caspian Sea alone wash its shores.

The second division of the fleet designed for hostile service in the Persian Gulf, rendezvoused at Bushire, otherwise named Bender Boshavir, one of the principal seaports of which we had possessed ourselves. It occupies the extremity of a peninsula twelve miles long, which high tides and storms render, at times, an island. The town, triangular in form, is fortified .by a mud wall armed with twelve pieces of cannon. Here the British flag was hoisted above the Persian lion, when the second division of the fleet sailed on the 19th of March, 1856, and joined the first division two days after at Ma'mer, an enlargement of the river, about twenty miles from its mouth.

General Havelock, who was second in command to Sir James Outram, was in command of the land forces, among which were the 78th Ross-shire Highlanders, an officer of whom, Captain G. H. Hunt, published an interesting narrative of the Persian campaign.

Cathcart's Hill

At Ma'mer a delay of two days ensued, while some necessary changes took place in the transports by shifting the troops and stores; and the whole fleet, on the 24th, with the troop-ships in tow steamed up the river without molestation from the Persians, and in the evening came to anchor opposite a thick tope or wood, four miles below the forts of Mohammerah, and in full view of them.

With their telescopes and field-glasses, many officers now went into the tops to reconnoitre, and by nine o'clock a boat with muffled oars, having on board some of the heads of departments, stole in shore to choose a position for a mortar battery, and actually crept close to the guns of Mohammerah, without being fired at, because quite unseen and unheard.

The night proved so dark, that unfortunately the officers on board could make little or no observation, and returned to the fleet without having affected their object.

On the evening of the 28th, the Persian Artillery, clad in blue surtouts with black fur caps, brought some field-pieces down to the ships, and opened fire chiefly on the Assaye, which, however, soon silenced them by her sixty-eight-pounders. They kept up a picket fire all night; and, as if in anticipation of our landing, bodies of their cavalry were visible, clad in light blue uniforms with white cross-belts, hovering among' the copse-wood that fringed the beach.

On the 26th, arrangements for the attack were complete by daylight in the morning. All the men-of-war had their steam up, and immediately after weighing anchor, each ship having an ensign flying at the head of every mast, proceeded to the strife in the following order : -

Feroze, with Commodore Young's broad pennant at the main; Semiramis, towing sloop Clive, of twelve guns; Assaye, Ajdaha, and Victoria, towing; Falkland, twelve guns ; meanwhile, all the transports, forming a squadron of fifty sailing-ships and steamers, remained at the anchorage until the fire of the batteries should be silenced.

At half-past six the Victoria and Falkland opened fire with their great guns, as an officer tells us, "on the blue-coated gentlemen before mentioned, who came down to have a quiet pot-shot at the ships as they passed, sending shell and grape into their ranks in fine style, and rolling them over like ninepins."

At seven a.m. the Feroze and Assaye having steamed into a good position about three hundred yards from 1 the forts, also opened fire, but with eighteen-inch shells. This was quickly and hotly returned by the Persians; while a mortar-raft which had been constructed, floored, and armed, on the preceding day was towed into position by the boats of the fleet, and threw 5.5 inch bombs into the enemy's works with splendid precision and deadly effect. In the meantime, the Ajdaha, Clive, Victoria, and Falkland, had taken up stations at 800 yards' distance, opening fire as they came up.

The sight was now magnificent, amid the beautiful scenery of the shore that bounded the Sea of Oman. The day was calm and sunny, and there was just breeze enough to blow the cloudlets of smoke clear of the ships, allowing a good and steady aim to be taken; hence very few shots were thrown away.

At eight o'clock the commodore ran up the signal for a closer attack the Victoria being the first ship up, from her light draught of water, took her station astern of the Assaye, and thus became the third ship in the line off the batteries. About two hundred yards from the mouth of the creek the water suddenly shoaled, and she grounded, thus becoming exposed to the concentrated fire of all the forts, and getting sorely battered in consequence.

Eighteen large round shots were buried in her hull, while much of her rigging was cut to pieces. In this exposed position she remained till noon, when the Feroze dropped down and drew some of the enemy's fire from her, while the Ajdaha, Semiramis, and the two sloops of war, came up at the same time, and the cannonade was maintained on both sides with great spirit.

At half-past twelve, the magazine of the north fort blew up with a terrible effect. Amid the dense column of smoke and dust that suddenly started skyward, there would be seen, for a moment, Persian corpses, horses' legs, huge pieces of mud, and bits of gun-carriages, all whirling together amid round shot and bursting shells, while a deafening cheer rang from ship to ship, and cannon and mortar were plied with greater vigour than ever.

Three other dreadful explosions followed this, and then the fire of the Persians began visibly to slacken. By two o'clock it had completely ceased; and then the Berenice, the river-steamers, and the steam transports, moving on past the silent and shattered batteries, soldiers and sailors cheering defiantly together, landed the troops of the expedition under General Havelock, covered by the guns of the Ajdaha. At the same time the northern forts were taken possession of, and the Union Jack

The Palace at Delhi

hoisted, one by the crew of the Assaye, the other by the crew of the Victoria.

At half-past two the enemy opened fire again, but with jingals and musketry only. To this the fleet responded with grape and canister, sending them, in dreadful showers, right through the embrasures. For thirty minutes this work continued, till the boats' crews of the Falkland landed and carried the place by storm - the Persians flying before them like terrified children - their officers setting the first example.

With the exception of a fort of five guns amid some date-trees on the left bank of the Haffar Creek, the whole of these works, three in number, occupied a kind of peninsula between the creek and the Shat-el-Arab, or common estuary of the Euphrates and Tigris.

In their rear lay the town of Mohammerah and the fortified camp of the Persian army. The troops having landed, marched inward in quest of the latter; but the terror of the cannonade from the seaward had proved too much for the nerves of the enemy.

It was currently said that when the ships opened fire, the Shahzadeh - uncle to the Persian monarch - sent three officers of rank from his camp to the forts in front to deliver some orders - one was killed, and another returned severely wounded and all over blood, while the third brought back a sixty-eight-pound shot

"Oh!" said the Shahzadeh, "if they are firing such things as that, we had better be off!"

Thus Havelock got quiet possession of the camp, tents, and clothing, without resistance, the valiant Shahzadeh, with 21,000 men, having vanished "like the baseless fabric of a vision," and the town, though heavy guns were on it, was taken with insignificant loss.

An officer of the Indian Navy describes the scene within

the captured forts as most revolting. Disemboweled, torn, and mangled, the bodies of men and horses were piled together amid broken and dismounted guns, powder-cases, arms, and gouts of blood. Many of the Persians lay there with their awful shell-wounds exposed to the burning sun, to the battening insects, and the whirling dust.

Thirty pieces of cannon, which had been thrown into nullahs and secret places by the fugitive enemy, were taken; and one more was found by an expedition consisting of the river - steamers under Acting Commodore Rennie, who ascended to Awaz, came up with the retreating army, and routed it, at the same time blowing up a magazine and taking an immense supply of grain and many mules, with which he returned.

"Yesterday, the 5th April," writes an officer of the Company's sea service, "we heard that the preliminaries of peace had been signed j and I think that, from the general and commodore down to the drummer-boy and messenger, every one is sorry for it, as no one thinks that they - the Persians - have had enough of English antibilious pills in the shape of lead and iron; and the idea that, after taking so much trouble to obtain possession, we are to evacuate entirely both Bushire and Mohammerah, makes every one savage."

Further operations being checked by intelligence of peace between Her Majesty and the Shah, who had sued for peace, the British troops returned to India, where their presence was soon indispensably required. On the 15th May, 1857, Brigadier General Havelock embarked with his staff in the steamer Berenice, and, after touching at Muscat, landed at Bombay on the 29th of the same month.

MORE FROM THE SAME SERIES

Most books from the 'Military History from Original Sources' series are edited and endorsed by
Emmy Award winning film maker and military historian Bob Carruthers, producer of Discovery
Channel's Line of Fire and Weapons of War and BBC's Both Sides of the Line. Long experience
and strong editorial control gives the military history enthusiast the ability to buy with confidence.
The series advisor is David McWhinnie, producer of the acclaimed Battlefield series for Discovery
Channel. David and Bob have co-produced books and films with a wide variety of the UK's leading
historians including Professor John Erickson and Dr David Chandler.
Where possible the books draw on rare primary sources to give the military enthusiast new insights
into a fascinating subject.

The English Civil Wars	The Zulu Wars	Into Battle with Napoleon 1812	Waterloo 1815
The Anglo-Saxon Chronicle	Medieval Warfare	Renaissance Warfare	1914-1918
Sea Battles in the Age of Sail	Sun Tzu - The Art of War	Recollections of the Great War in the Air	Soldier of the Empire

For more information visit www.pen-and-sword.co.uk